San

Past, Present, & Always

Mel Brown

Schiffer Publishing Ltd

4880 Lower Valley Road, Atglen, Pennsylvania 19310

This modern postcard shows downtown San Antonio, as seen from the Tower of the Americas around 2002. Construction of new hotels along the River Walk and key midtown locations sees new structures on a larger scale than older buildings. Larger hotels are now being added as the old city center renews itself and tourism keeps downtown busy. *Circa 2000, $1.*

Other Schiffer Books on Related Subjects:
Greetings from San Antonio,
978-0-7643-2679-0, $24.95
Greetings from Dallas,
978-0-7643-2805-3, $19.95
Ghosts of Fort Worth:
Investigating Cowtown's Most Haunted,
978-0-7643-2813-8, $14.95

Schiffer Books are available at special discounts for bulk purchases for sales promotions or premiums. Special editions, including personalized covers, corporate imprints, and excerpts can be created in large quantities for special needs. For more information contact the publisher:

Schiffer Publishing Ltd.
4880 Lower Valley Road
Atglen, PA 19310
Phone: (610) 593-1777
Fax: (610) 593-2002
E-mail: Info@schifferbooks.com

For the largest selection of fine reference books on this and related subjects, please visit our web site at:
www.schifferbooks.com
We are always looking for people to write books on new and related subjects. If you have an idea for a book please contact us at the above address.

This book may be purchased from the publisher. Include $5.00 for shipping. Please try your bookstore first. You may write for a free catalog.

In Europe, Schiffer books are distributed by:
Bushwood Books
6 Marksbury Ave.
Kew Gardens
Surrey TW9 4JF England
Phone: 44 (0) 20 8392-8585
Fax: 44 (0) 20 8392-9876
E-mail: info@bushwoodbooks.co.uk
Website: **www.bushwoodbooks.co.uk**

Free postage in the U.K., Europe; air mail at cost.

Here is a typical sidewalk Real Photo Post Card (RPPC) that was taken in May 1940 of my mother-to-be, the then eighteen-year-old Kathleen Meads, and her mother Bessie who was a nurse at the nearby Nix Hospital. A photographer caught them on East Houston Street as they had passed the popular MANHATTAN Cafe next door to the Majestic Theater. *Circa 1940, $4-8.*

This copper print postcard of downtown San Antonio was made in the early 1900s. The photograph was taken from the old fortress like Post Office on Alamo Plaza looking southwest past the large Alamo Fire Insurance Building towards the Bexar County Courthouse. The Insurance company fronted on Navarro Street partly where La Mansion Hotel is now. This card's backside featured a price list for postcard publishing that gives a good idea of what costs were at that time for businesses wanting to advertise by mail. *Circa 1904, $4-5.*

Birds Eye View of San Antonio, Texas, looking west from Post Office

Place Stamp Here
Domestic One cent
Foreign Two cents

POST CARD

Sample from S. Langsdorf & Co. 13-17 Crosby Street, New York, N. Y.

Copper Print Execution.

No. 117. S. Langsdorf & Co., New York. — Germany

Prices.
In Lots of 1000 of one Subject only $9.00 per 1000 Cards.
.... 2000 .... $8.00
.... 3000 .... $7.50
.... 5000 .... $7.00
..............10.000 .... $6.75

THIS SIDE IS FOR THE ADDRESS ONLY

....10.000 ....

E IS FOR THE ADDRESS ONLY

nly $9.00 per 1
... $8.00 ......
... $7.50 ......
... $7.00 ......
... $6.75 ......

Preface

San Antonio, Texas is my hometown and one of the most historic cites in North America. This book is a companion to an earlier one from Schiffer Publishing, Ltd., *Greetings from San Antonio*, published in June 2007, but mine has a much different emphasis thematically and a novel focus in imagery. Authors Mary L. Martin and Nathaniel Wolfgang-Price did a fine job of providing the reader a solid foundation for the general history of the old "Alamo City" from its beginning in 1718 until the 1940s by using more than three hundred vintage postcards. This book, *San Antonio: Past, Present & Always*, will give readers a more personal look at the colorful town based on my recollections as a fourth generation San Antonian whose family's roots there go back to the start of the 1880s. This will be achieved through the use of more than three hundred images from vintage and modern postcards, a few rare archival photos, and modern snapshots.

One particularly special type of old postcard prominent in this collection is the "Real Photo Post Card" or the RPPC, as photo historians and collectors now know it. This style of postcard was promoted by the Kodak Company in 1903 as a way to popularize its new No. 3A Folding Pocket Camera, which shot a 3-1/2" x 5-1/2" size image that could be printed with a postcard back upon request. Other cameras were also used to make personal photo type postcards, but beginning in 1907 Kodak offered a printing service that allowed any negative to be printed as a postcard. This film service was then used by serious or amateur photographers to shoot ordinary people and places made noteworthy by an event or occurrence. Man-made or natural disasters, wars, catastrophes, and historic occasions were increasingly caught on film thanks to the RPPC's availability and popularity.

A perfect example are the RPPCs herein that document San Antonio's floods of the early twentieth century. They were not commercially viable as tourist postcards, but were popular among city residents and were printed by the dozen rather than by the thousands. Other Real Photo cards were made throughout the years of the Alamo on unique occasions or special anniversaries, but again not in high volume like ordinary color postcards for typical tourist sales. This type of card could be made by almost anyone with a decent camera, a good eye, and who happened to be at the right place at the right time. Many of those now deemed to be the most collectable seemed to have been produced by professionals or serious hobbyists who knew a good subject when they saw it. Some collectors today now seek out only the images of certain photographers, which has driven the values of those cards up regardless of their subject.

RPPC subjects included main streets in small towns, school buildings, courthouses, social clubs and gatherings, or anything else that caught the photographer's eye. Small businesses were good to catch on film because the owner/operator could use the card for advertising. RPPCs also included views of people walking along busy downtown sidewalks that were taken by street photographers in cities across America.

Real Photo Post Cards are also frequently among the rarest, expensive, most sought after collectable of all postal mailed cards just because they were often printed in relatively small batches. Companies such as Curt Teich of Chicago or Dexter Press in Ohio printed cards in the thousands or hundreds of thousands of certain well-known tourist sites. Common color San Antonio postcards of the Alamo, River Walk, Courthouse, other missions, parks and downtown streets for example are relatively easy to find and are low in price. Some RPPCs are often uniquely important due to the historic significance of the moment in time that they captured; sometimes they are the only record to be found of such an event, moment, or person.

Another out of the ordinary type postcard included here is the Art Card. These are simply those postcards whose images are not photographic, but original art reproductions on a small scale. I have been publishing limited numbers of my own paintings this way for years, as have other artists. Not aimed at tourists usually, these cards are more typically sold in gift shops, exhibitions, and trade shows.

Another feature of this book is found in its theme of *Past, Present, & Always*. Here I have attempted to juxtapose an archival postcard with either a modern card or a personal photo taken recently to show what change, if any, has occurred to that building or location. There has been great change in some instances while others show little change for better or worse. In some cases there is almost no change to be seen. I have also included, as often as was possible, personal memories to the card views in hopes that the reader will be entertained as well as educated about some aspect of the old town.

Since the authors of *Greetings from San Antonio* did such a good job of covering the popular or familiar aspects of the city, I have chosen to take a different approach to the subject. They showed us the Alamo as seen in several common cards while I have been lucky enough to gather rare or unusual views of the historic old mission/fort. Also included are views of "the other Alamos"—ones of movie fame or those located elsewhere. The first San Antonio book gave us the early views of the now famous River Walk while I have included some modern cards that show it as it is today—a place still seen by millions of delighted tourists each year. I have also added several RPPC views showing the catastrophic history of the pretty little river that destroyed much of downtown once or twice a decade until the 1930s.

Contents

Introduction

San Antonio was long ago named one of the "four unique cities" in the United States along with Boston, San Francisco, and New Orleans because of its colorful history and all-American blend of diverse ethnic cultures. Coahuiltecan Indians, known as Payayas, called their springs and village here Yanaguana. This city would not exist if there were no water flowing from the springs north of downtown just beyond Brackenridge Park. Arrowheads over 10,000 years old have been discovered at the San Antonio Springs, located behind the University of the Incarnate Word.

Indigenous tribes were the first human users of this ancient water source that eventually brought Europeans to the area. Some historians believe Alonso de Leon, a relative of Ponce de Leon, was the first white man to camp at the river's headwaters in 1670. The small but prolific waterway has a long and interesting history made more important by the city that shares its name and fame. This little river is the reason that San Antonio is on the "four unique cities" list as it continues to bring life to the people who live here.

New Orleans may not be on that list today, but ironically its own catastrophic flooding by Hurricane Rita in 2005 reminded us that San Antonio's unique character is due in large part to similarly terrific floods on a smaller scale. More ironic perhaps is the fact that New Orleans inspired the man responsible for designing the "river park" theme that has made the Alamo City famous as an "American Venice."

Robert Hugman was a native San Antonian who had lived in New Orleans four years before returning to his hometown to develop what became the renowned River Walk. He had been inspired by the old Creole city on the Mississippi that was well known for its dedication to preserving and conserving its own natural beauty and cultural charms. Hugman brought those concepts back to San Antonio just when they were most needed.

For decades the little river that runs through it had brought death and destruction to downtown San Antonio on an increasingly large scale as the city grew. Its continued urban metamorphosis was directly linked to the frequent floods that occurred too regularly on the small but confined river that begins a few miles north of downtown. The former frontier town on the edge of the Texas Hill Country saw rapid growth beginning with the arrival of the railroad in 1877.

With each passing decade of economic growth the San Antonio River and its urban tributaries such as the San Pedro and Alazan Creeks became ever more restricted in their abilities to shed water during the sometimes heavy rains generated by storms in the Gulf of Mexico or coming directly out of Mexico from the Pacific. In September 1921 one such deluge happened, killing dozens of citizens and putting some downtown streets under nearly ten feet of water. Public outcry finally moved the city fathers to act and Robert Hugman was one of those hired to alleviate the problem.

This was not easily done, and took many years and millions of dollars to realize. So the modern "river park" was born of the need to stabilize and control a narrow, shallow, spring-fed stream that happened to run through the very heart of a blossoming urban metropolis. To solve the problem some straightening and widening of the natural riverbed was managed. A few miles north of downtown, Olmos Dam was built to contain runoff upstream that fed directly into the actual springs behind Incarnate Word College. Secondary development came later that brought about the actual River Walk as it is recognized today. The end result was miles of beautifully landscaped sidewalks and bridges connecting the dozens of shops, cafes, and hotels that give San Antonio its truly unique character and romantic ambiance. Along with the city's five historic Spanish missions, this downtown waterway and surrounding environment give the city its special feel and flavor.

Naturally there is more to the old town than its birthright wellspring and "Outpost of the Empires" legacy. This book's other chief focus is on San Antonio's long and illustrious role in American military history. As much as downtown has always been the heart of the city, another singular component in San Antonio's makeup has long been the equally historic military presence here. Begun as a garrison town by the Spanish along their important and strategic *Camino Real* or King's Highway, this city has always seen more men and women in uniform than just about any other city in the United States. The U.S. Army first arrived in 1845 when Texas became the twenty-eighth state. It still maintains two major facilities here; Fort Sam Houston was established in 1870 and in 1916 the 12,000-acre Camp Bullis was created in northern Bexar County. Sprawling Camp Bullis continues to be a training facility for the Army despite being increasingly surrounded by city growth. Fort Sam, as it is known locally, with its Brooke General Medical Center, is the largest and most important military medical training facility in the world.

In 1910 Fort Sam became home to the Army's first pilots and their "aeroplanes" as America's military air arm began its historic development. By 1916-1917 Kelly and Brooks Fields were established to train flyers and then in 1930 Randolph Field was opened and became the "West Point of the Air." During World War II a fourth installation named the San Antonio Aviation Cadet Center was created. In 1948 that site became Lackland Air Force Base and was dedicated to provide incoming recruits their initial or "Basic Training." Approximately seven million young men and women have passed through Lackland since 1948 when it became the sole basic training site for America's uniformed aerospace component. The Air Force story alone could fill a large book, but herein is a much-condensed look at this history through vintage postcards and archival imagery.

Beautiful San Antonio River

San Antonio's well-known and much enjoyed River Walk helped transform the flood prone urban stream beginning around 1930. The Navarro Street Bridge's lovely curves have always been a favorite of photographers and tourists alike. This view includes one of the quaint Venetian style gondolas that were briefly popular on the river in the late 1950s-early 1960s. *Circa 1960, $2-5.*

Chapter One

River of Life

"River of Life" well describes the ancient waterway because without it there would be no city named for the patron saint of "things lost." The Payaya Indians, who had lived here for centuries before the Spanish arrived, called the river Yanaguana or "Drunken old man going home at night" because it rambled as it went downstream. Archaeologists believe the original site of San Antonio has known human life for at least 10,000 years and that is simply because of the river that always flows. Its modern history is one of turmoil both natural and man-made, but without it there would be no San Antonio. Flooding had long been a problem that went unsolved until the twentieth century. The resulting fix was not to merely control the river's path, but to enhance it into a thing of beauty that combines its natural flow with engineered elegance. More hotels, restaurants, clubs, and attractions were built as downtown shifted from being a retail to a tourist mecca. Then ironically a mall was born on the river walk itself.

Olmos Dam was completed in 1926 at a cost of over 1.5 million dollars and was the first major step in controlling the river during periods of heavy rain on the city's north side. It sits astride the Olmos Basin just above the ancient San Antonio Springs and can be seen immediately east of I-37 North. *Circa 1940, $3-5.*

11:—OLMAS DAM, SAN ANTONIO, TEXAS

12:-SKYLINE, SAN ANTONIO, TEXAS

This view was taken from atop the Pioneer Flour Mills and shows the city's modern skyline. Following the trauma of World War II, San Antonio began to see more growth. It had become a major metropolitan center but was no longer the largest city in Texas as it had been for many years. Its quaintly winding river, by then modernized, was now a tourist destination in its own right. *Circa 1950, $3-5.*

Old Mill Bridge

Dec 4 - 1913

Before large-scale flood control projects were started with completion of the Olmos Dam in 1926, this scene was a reality every few years. Printed on a RPPC, the deluge is especially impressive when compared with the serene views taken later of the picturesque little river. There is now a Works Progress Administration (WPA) tile plaque at the site that commemorates the "Old Mill Crossing," which was the historic ford used before the bridge was erected. *Dated Dec. 4- 1913, $14-30.*

Similar flooding caught on film barely a month earlier in 1913 causes one to wonder why anyone lived or invested in downtown San Antonio before flood control. College Street ran only three short blocks just north of the Saint Mary's, Navarro and North Presa Streets bridges so the river was nearby. *RPPC dated Sept. 21, 1913, $14-30.*

College St. Oct 1913

PONTOON BOAT ST. MARYS ST SEPT. 21 - LOOKING N

GUNTER HOT

The high water mark on this North St. Mary's Street building is well over ten feet, judging by the man standing under the sign. This meant that the ground floor of nearly every building in downtown San Antonio was under several feet of water depending on its nearness to the river itself. *RPPC circa 1913, $14-30.*

Alazan Creek runs through San Antonio's west side and, before Olmos Dam and other flood control fixes were put in place, always had the worst flooding outside of downtown. This RPPC shows the half-mile wide deluge that swept away many homes near Alazan Creek in October 1913. *Circa 1913, $14-30.*

A second view of the serious flooding done by Alazan Creek shows how wide the flooded area could be. Really effective control of west side floods was not managed until the 1950s and 1960s. It was finally accomplished with massive concrete channels and dams built to move the large body of water sometimes experienced. *RPPC dated October 23, 1913, $11-20.*

The Southwestern Telegraph and Telephone Company opened the first exchange in San Antonio in 1881 and some years later built this modern six-story structure at 215 East Travis Street next to Fire Station #2. Atop the firehouse is the then typical watchtower used for visibly spotting smoke and fire around town. *Circa 1920, $09-15.*

Telephone Building and Central Fire Station, San Antonio, Texas.

October 1913 also saw downtown under water. The new telephone exchange had its ground floor flooded thus trapping several dozen operators on the upper floors of the building. One of these early operators was 17-year-old Nell Agnes Edwards who, many years later, became my grandmother. She loved telling the story of being carried down a ladder into rescue boats by a handsome fireman during the big flood of 1913. *RPPC dated October 1913, $14-30.*

Since 1946 Casa Rio Mexican Restaurant has offered tourists and locals good food and boat rentals on the River Walk next to the Commerce Street Bridge. This gondola style boat was picturesque but impractical so lasted only a few years. *Circa 1960, $5-7*

Another view of Casa Rio on East Commerce Street again shows the covered gondola type river boats that the restaurant rented to tourists. *Circa 1960, $5-7. Courtesy of Craig Covner.*

This more recent card shows the modern barge type river craft now used to carry tourists. Here one makes the turn around the raised stage at Rivercenter Mall on the latest part of the River Walk to be built. *Circa 2000, $1-2.*

12

Arneson River Theater   San Antonio, Texas

Nix Hospital looms in the far background of this Arneson River Theater view. Dozens of performances are staged here each year for audiences across the river on La Villita's grassy amphitheater type seating. *Circa 1990, $1-2.*

Yolanda

A barge named Yolanda carries its human cargo toward the Commerce Street Bridge and the Hilton Palacio del Rio. Another barge makes the turn into the newest part of the river, which was added to access the Rivercenter Mall that opened in 1988. *Circa 1990, $1-2.*

RIVERWALK
SAN ANTONIO

Casa Rio feeds nighttime visitors out for a good time at the many nightclubs and music venues along the River Walk, which is transformed by creative lighting. Circa 2000, $1-2.

Postcard companies sometimes did weird things in their art departments to "enhance" a card's marketability—and this night view of the Transit Tower is a good example. It never was lit like this in its lifetime thank goodness and one wonders how popular this card was. *Circa 1935, $3-6.*

In an idyllic view, the beautiful 1927 Smith-Young Tower, on a 1940s linen card, shows off its stylish relationship with the river in the days before the River Walk was created. This unforgettable landmark structure sits beside the river that made the city. *Circa 1940, $2-4.*

Made about 1960, this neat card looks south along Saint Mary's Street from East Martin Street toward the ever prominent Transit Tower some nine blocks away through the heart of downtown. On the immediate left is the Greyhound Bus Station, which is still there, and the once regal Bluebonnet Hotel that is now gone. The Hotel Lanier was next, but it is also now gone. The always-elegant Gunter Hotel sits in the next block. Opened in 1909, the historic Sheraton Gunter is alive and well, but the others have all vanished including the little Hotel Nueces and larger Builder's Exchange Building on the right, as the city's center continues to change. *Circa 1960, $8-10.*

14

The 1891 built Clifford Building continues to watch over the Commerce Street bridge section of the river as another barge glides past in recent years. *Circa 2000, $1-2.*

Here is the "Tower Life" building as of today; standing just as tall and majestic as always but no longer the highest building in town as it had been when opened and until 1986. It has an elegance unlike any other and continues to capture the imagination.

SAN ANTONIO RIVER SHOWING COMMERCE ST. BRIDGE.

By the early 1900s the city fathers began to modernize the river as it ran through downtown. This charming view looks south toward the Commerce Street Bridge and shows off the new landscaping done along the riverbank to improve its aesthetic appeal to visitors and residents alike. *Circa 1920, $2-4.*

Landscaping did produce more pleasing scenes along the old river but did little to stop the occasional flooding. Still the new look made great postcards like this one. *Circa 1924, $2-4.*

Warmly glowing candles in sand filled bags means Fiesta de las Luminarias that lines River Walk as a symbolic "lighting of the way" for the Holy Family. A centuries old tradition, it begins at dusk on Friday then again on Saturday and Sunday nights only. The Tower of the Americas becomes a giant candle itself. *Circa 2000, $1-2*

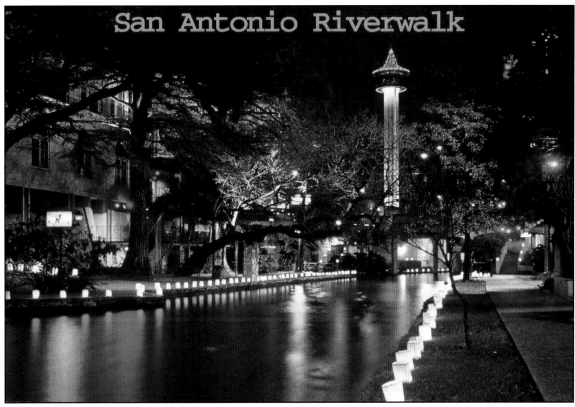

16

Sing Chong Company 124 S. Pecos San Antonio Tex. 4/9/1910

A little recognized feature of San Antonio is its historic Chinese community which began arriving with the Southern Pacific Railroad in 1881 that many of them helped build. At first most Chinese settled into the West side Hispanic neighborhoods and operated grocery stores like the Sing Chong Company seen here. Because of its mainly Hispanic clientele the store's motto was "Ventas por Mayor y Menor" as can be seen on the wall behind the counter. It meant "Sales large and small" as these merchants were very competitive. *Dated 4-9-1910, $14-20. Courtesy of Fred & Rose Wong.*

Chapter Two:
Chinese Heart of Texas

An often-overlooked ethnic minority community in San Antonio's long history were the Chinese. Many of the most common older historical, place, and street names in the Alamo City are either Hispanic or German with other ethnic groups filling in the gaps. Except for the temporary renaming of a well-known park feature, the Chinese have been all but invisible here so now is the time to catch up on their history. They have been a vital part of San Antonio since the 1880s, but always in the background just getting by and going along simply as regular Americans beholding to no one. My wife is Chinese American so maybe that makes me a bit more sensitive to their story, but it's a great story — so here is a little bit of it in postcards.

This Christmas Hong Kong Market RPPC from 1939 shows one of the city's many Chinese mom and pop grocery stores. By that time there were dozens spread across the near suburbs as the Chinese American community grew. *Dated 12-20-1939, $9-12. Courtesy of Virginia Wong.*

LIBERTY FOOD STORE Grand Opening 3403 South Flores St. April 20, 1941

World War I U.S. Army veteran Pon Tong Wong opened his own grocery in April 1941 with his family living upstairs as was typical then. Oldest son Frank took over when his father passed away in 1967 and Liberty Food Store operated at 3403 South Flores Street until 1998. *Dated April 20, 1941, $9-12. Courtesy of Frank Wong.*

By the 1930s the Grant Hotel on West Commerce had become a kind of mini-Chinatown in that it was home to dozens of Chinese. This included several of the aging Pershing Chinese from Mexico and young families. Signs on the building's side stated "Live and Let Live," which was Grant's motto and "Beds from .50 cents. Cots .25 cents." *Circa 1930, $14-20. Courtesy of Mamie Lew.*

The Grant Hotel's street level was filled in part by the BOW LIM Meat Market & Grocery operated by Mr. Louie Lim. The large, modern and well-stocked market offered a wide variety of goods and most importantly it had an up to date meat market. That was a time when most homes still had "ice boxes" instead of electric refrigeration. *Circa 1930, $14-20. Courtesy of Mamie Lew.*

Another of the more modern Chinese American markets was the Sang Wah at 1402 North Zaramora and Menchaca Streets. Located just northwest of downtown it was one of nearly one hundred Chinese American businesses around town most of them being groceries and meat markets. The old building is still there on the corner, but is now a boxing club and gymnasium. *Circa 1942, $8-10. Courtesy of Sam K. Eng.*

SANG WAH Co. Meat Market & Groceries
1402 N. Zarzamora St. San Antonio-Tex.
Tel. PE 8173

This old brick two-story at 215 South San Saba Street became the San Antonio Chinese School in 1927 when Chinese community leaders opened it for their children. The kids attended public school each day and then here, in the evenings, they were taught traditional Chinese language, history, culture, and art. *Circa 1930, $8-10. Courtesy of Mary Eng.*

Here are some of the ABC girls, the American-Born Chinese, behind the old school building where there was an outhouse still in use in 1935. *Dated Sept. 9-1937, $8-10. Courtesy of Sam K. Eng.*

This postwar image was taken on the Chinese School's steps with the entire class gathered. All ages attended as seen here with high school teenagers down to first and second graders present. *Circa 1947, $8-10. Courtesy of Sam K. Eng.*

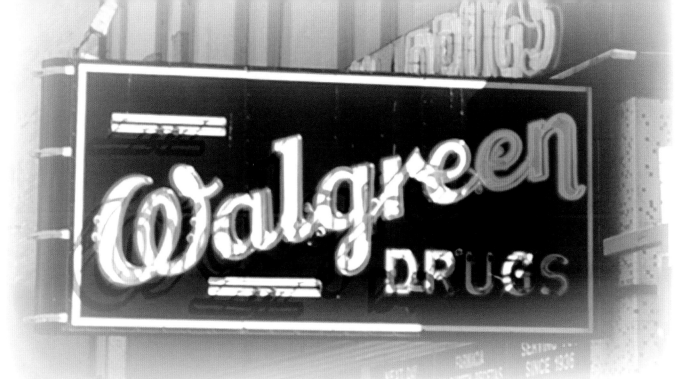

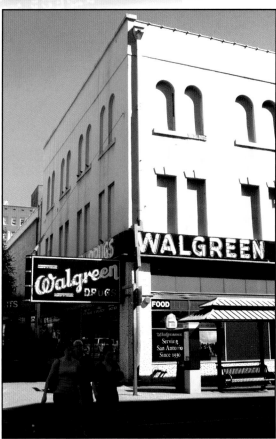

The classic neon signs are still there in October of 2007 as the old Walgreen Pharmacy on Houston Street at Navarro survives. It no longer has a soda fountain/lunch counter, but is one of very few old time businesses still in downtown San Antonio.

A street photographer caught Home Service volunteers Toy May Leung and Francis Wong during a march early on in World War II as they moved along East Houston Street past the Walgreen Pharmacy at Navarro. *Circa 1942, $8-10. Courtesy of Sam K. Eng.*

Rice Bowl Parade
10-10-'41   SanAntonio,Tx.

War in China began in 1937 when the Japanese military invaded years before they attacked Pearl Harbor. San Antonio's Chinese community and clubs sponsored parades to raise funds for the "Rice Bowl." Here Naomi Leung leads a China Relief group on horseback down Avenue E past the Medical Arts Building and Post Office toward Alamo Plaza. *Dated 10-10-1941, $8-10. Courtesy of Sam K. Eng.*

Marchers followed Naomi on foot carrying banners and portraits of Gen. Chiang Kai-shek and President Franklin Roosevelt to signify unity between the two nations. *Circa 1942, $8-10. Courtesy of Sam K. Eng.*

Rice Bowl Parade
10-10.'41 San Antonio.Tx.

Naomi's brother John Leung leads a group of men pulling a large paper mache bowl for bystanders to toss money into for the "Rice Bowl" project. This money went to buy tons of rice for the starving villagers back home where many San Antonio Chinese still had relatives. *Dated 10-10-1941, $8-10. Courtesy of Sam K. Eng.*

The Young Chinese League (YCL) began in 1945 as a club for the youthful members of the community. Many of them had been born in Texas or elsewhere in the United States and were known as ABCs or American Born Chinese. Making floats for the annual Fiesta Parades was a favorite effort each spring as seen in this RPPC shot at the Fiesta finale Flambeau or night parade. During the 1950s and 1960s most of the floats featured the FREE CHINA theme as an anti-communist Red China message. *Circa 1955, $8-10. Courtesy of Virginia Wong.*

This YCL float was titled "Festive Moon" as it moved along on its flatbed tractor-trailer. Club members did all the hard work each year sometimes winning prizes for their efforts. In 1995 many of the original Young Chinese League members gathered for a 50th anniversary reunion in San Antonio. *Circa 1960, $8-10. Courtesy of Virginia Wong.*

John Leung 555th ASG. Chihkiang 7-2-'45

Sgt. John Leung sits in the cargo door of a C-47 Sky train transport at Chihkiang Air Base, China, in the summer of 1945. As a member of the all Chinese-American 555th Air Service Squadron, he provided ground support for fighter, bomber, and cargo units operating against Japanese forces in central China. *Dated 7-2-1945, $8-10. Courtesy of Dora Leung.*

Frank Eng. Stinson Field   1-15-'39

Pvt. Sam Wong - First Jump Fort Bragg, North Carolina 9-3-1941

Private Sam Wong of San Antonio makes his first parachute jump from an airplane in October 1941 at Fort Bragg, North Carolina. He had joined the 82nd Airborne Division, which jumped into North Africa in November 1942 as part of Operation Torch to defeat Nazi forces there. In September 1943 his unit was dropped behind enemy lines in Italy where he and others were captured after two weeks of combat. He then became a Prisoner of War until the Germans surrendered in May 1945. *Dated 9-3-1941, $8-10. Courtesy of Sam Wong.*

This great RPPC shows Frank Eng with his very unusual Pitcairn Autogyro at Stinson Field in January of 1939. Frank was an experienced pilot who had flown the mail before the airlines started doing it and became a civilian pilot instructor during World War II. *Dated 1-15-1939, $8-10. Courtesy of Connie Eng.*

JOHN L's Cafe
715 Nogalitos at Zavala St.
PE 5-8573

After World War II John Leung returned to San Antonio, and with his wife Dora, opened a small grocery store at 715 Nogalitos Street and Zavala. Dora's homemade tamales and chili became store favorites so they remodeled the store into an eatery named John L's Cafe. *Circa 1975, $8-10. Courtesy of Dora Leung.*

WW II / 82nd Airborne veteran Sam Wong opened BIG TOWN Hardware on Old Laredo Highway in 1949 and closed it in 2004. Sam grew up working in his father's Sing Chong Company on West Commerce Street before the war. Sam and his wife Edna also had a motel next door to BIG TOWN for many years.

24

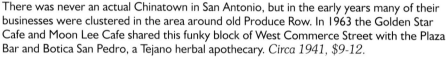

There was never an actual Chinatown in San Antonio, but in the early years many of their businesses were clustered in the area around old Produce Row. In 1963 the Golden Star Cafe and Moon Lee Cafe shared this funky block of West Commerce Street with the Plaza Bar and Botica San Pedro, a Tejano herbal apothecary. *Circa 1941, $9-12.*

Chinese American grocery stores once dotted the city landscape with nearly a hundred of them by 1960. Historically they were a good though hard way to make a living, raise a family and even prosper a bit. The Jan Woo Grocery out on West Commerce Street appears to be the last one left since the later generations have preferred higher education to competing with HEB or Super Wal-Mart.

The Lim family's Golden Star Cafe at 821 West Commerce Street has been in San Antonio since the mid 1930s. This makes it the oldest Chinese eatery and one of the oldest continually operating restaurants in the city. Urban renewal pushed them out and around over the years, this being their third location. Well known for placing chop suey, egg foo young with tacos and enchiladas on the same plate if ordered, the most popular menu is Item # 99 Deep Fried Fish with brown gravy, a family secret.

The elegant Tai Shan Chinese Restaurant at 2611 Broadway Street opened its doors in 1946 at a cost of over $100,000. The city's largest and fanciest Chinese restaurant at the time was opened as a joint venture by local businessman and civic leader Mr. Ted Wu. *Circa 1958, $5-7*

This interior view of Tai Shan's elegant dining room shows off the modern decor and fine bone china on linen tablecloths. A large wait staff made the Tai Shan's reputation second to none for many years. *Circa 1952, $2-3*

The classy Tai Shan closed in 1990 and sat empty for nearly a decade. In 2000 the building was renovated and is now home to the Fiesta San Antonio Commission that oversees the annual citywide celebration each April known as Fiesta Week.

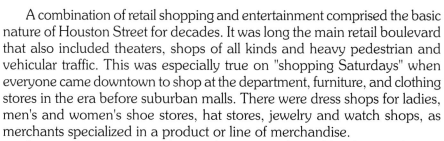

Chapter Three:

Main Street and More

A combination of retail shopping and entertainment comprised the basic nature of Houston Street for decades. It was long the main retail boulevard that also included theaters, shops of all kinds and heavy pedestrian and vehicular traffic. This was especially true on "shopping Saturdays" when everyone came downtown to shop at the department, furniture, and clothing stores in the era before suburban malls. There were dress shops for ladies, men's and women's shoe stores, hat stores, jewelry and watch shops, as merchants specialized in a product or line of merchandise.

It was also a street with popular eating places like the Manhattan Cafe and the lunch counters found in the various "variety stores" such as Woolworth's, Neisners, and Kresses. Those were the so-called Five and Dime Stores that had everything imaginable from parakeets and fish to toys, basic garments, household goods, and many other items of low cost as America's middle class was growing following the Great Depression and World War II. Sides streets running across Houston were also populated with these specialty stores and eateries with places like the Coney Island Hot-Dog shop, Percherniks' Sporting Goods, Alamo Hobby Shop, candy stores, and movie houses like the Empire and Prince. I wish there were postcards for many of these places too, but, sadly, there do not seem to be.

The downtown was beginning to feel its age by the mid 1960s as older nearby neighborhoods fell into neglect and new suburbs spread farther out. A large area bordered by South Alamo and East Commerce Streets had fallen from grace, was condemned as urban blight, demolished, and then rebuilt as Hemis Fair in 1968. That less than totally successful experiment in socio-cultural engineering had a huge and still reverberating effect on the heart of downtown. It marked the beginning of downtown's renaissance of tourism and vitality. Even though the Fair lasted only six months, it sparked a revitalization of the city center that continues today. Some older large office buildings are gaining a new lease on life as modern hotels and the ever-expanding freeway system makes getting around town easier and more efficient.

Houston Street at Night   San Antonio, Texas

This panorama view at dusk shows all the same businesses now beginning to light up for nighttime shoppers and movie goers. Woolworth's variety store and Sommers Drugs across from it each had lunch counters always ready with milk shakes, banana splits, BLTs, hamburgers, or plate lunches. *Circa 1960, $6-9*

HOUSTON STREET, SAN ANTONIO, TEXAS—71

Looking east on Houston Street, there's the Texas and Majestic theaters on what was once the busiest street downtown. That ended when shopping malls came to the suburbs in the 1960s and retailers gradually closed their doors all over the city's center district. Multiplex cinemas followed the malls and the old movie palaces downtown closed too.
Circa 1935, $3-5.

Houston Street, Looking West, San Antonio, Texas.

FISCHER'S DRUG STORE

This early view westward down Houston Street dates back to 1900 when the original, fortress looking federal building/post office anchored Alamo Plaza's north end.
Circa 1909, $5-9

"The Broadway of San Antonio" was how the city thought of Houston Street for many years from the 1890s to the 1960s. It was considered the main retail shopping street running from Alamo Plaza west to San Pedro Creek.
Circa 1912, $6-8.

HOUSTON ST., LOOKING WEST, POST OFFICE IN FOREGROUND. THE BROADWAY OF SAN ANTONIO, TEX.

Fifty years later another photographer caught the still busy shopping strand. Looking down Houston Street to Jefferson Street, we see many dress shops, shoe stores, variety or five & dimes like the Kress & Co. The Majestic Theater is on the left showing the latest movies from Hollywood. Now nearly forgotten variety stores like W. T. Grant, Kress & Co., Woolworth's, Neisners, Ben Franklins, and specialty shops like Fombys, Vogue, Burt Shoes, Mission Jewelry, Sol Franks Uniforms, and Carl's Clothing were all familiar for many years when most shopping was done downtown. *Circa 1960, $5-8.*

A few hours later and it's nearly closing time for the many merchants along Houston Street as the downtown becomes a much different place. Shoppers went home, traffic thinned, and lights went out. *Circa 1965, $3-5.*

San Antonio, Texas

The Majestic Theater kept busy showing movies until well after midnight while most of downtown was quiet. On the left is the Hertzberg Jewelry Company's 1878 clock reading 8:20 p.m. The photographer stood at the corner of St. Mary's and East Houston Streets to take this neat shot. The old, cast iron, hand wound clock is still standing and keeping time courtesy of restoration prompted by the San Antonio Conservation Society. Across the street, above the Thom McAn shoe store, hung the large sign for the Empire Theater, which is still just around the corner, having also been restored in recent years. *Circa 1963, $5-7.*

San Antonio

Above the same intersection of Alamo and Houston Streets forty years later finds a San Antonio much changed except for the venerable Alamo lit up as always. This modern card looking south at sunset still shows light traffic after dark with two large hotels and the Tower of the Americas breaking the horizon. *Circa 2003, $1-2.*

30

The evocative afterglow in this dreamlike view silhouettes the always-perfect Transit Tower and stolid old Alamo National Bank building with its brightly salient temperature gauge jutting skyward. *Circa 1969, $2-3.*

Even this familiar old River Walk scene is a bit spooky without people or activity. This card was wholly created in the card company's art department using a standard daylight view. *Circa 1940, $2-3.*

CORNER OF MEZZANINE PROMENADE, AZTEC THEATRE, SAN ANTONIO, TEXAS

INTERSTATE CIRCUIT, INC.

Most of the people downtown at night in the good old days were inside one of the classic movie palaces like the Majestic or Aztec seen here. This view of the Mayan, Toltec, Aztec-influenced mezzanine decor is still impressive to see anywhere and especially inside a movie theater. *Circa 1940, $6-8. Courtesy of J. Griffis Smith/Tx.DoT.*

The menacing Aztec snake sits in the lobby's center under the restored chandelier first hung in 1926. *Circa 2006, $2-4. Courtesy of J. Griffis Smith/Tx.DoT.*

After many years of decline and as multiplex screens opened in the suburbs, the Aztec Theater finally closed in 1984. Thanks to the San Antonio Conservation Society the Aztec reopened in May 2006 fully restored. This view of the incredible lobby shows the exotic Mayan theme decor magically lit. *Circa 2006, $2-4. Courtesy of J. Griffis Smith/Tx.DoT.*

32

The dramatically ornate Majestic auditorium was built with an artful blend of Baroque, Spanish Mission, and Mediterranean motifs that is still a wonder to experience. The classic theater featured many of the nation's most prominent actors, singers, bands and vaudevillians of the day along with the movies that were also screened. *Circa 1940, $4-6.*

INTERIOR, MAJESTIC THEATRE, SAN ANTONIO, TEXAS

As home to the San Antonio Symphony, the Majestic now also hosts a variety of live stage performances including Broadway musicals, TV comedians, and well known country or rock bands. Here is the spacious lobby following restoration with ornate ceiling and chandelier. *Circa 1990, $4-6. Courtesy of J. Griffis Smith/Tx.DoT.*

MANHATTAN CAFE - San Antonio, Texas

Beginning in the late 1920s and for many years thereafter the Manhattan Cafe sat next door to the Majestic Theater preparing meals for hungry movie goers and others twenty-four hours a day. It had long been a busy eatery but closed about the same time the theater next door did. *Circa 1940, $6-7.*

This "birdseye" view was taken from the Victoria Plaza Apartments for senior citizens on Barrera Street several blocks southeast of downtown. The cameraman looked northwest and caught the Refugio and Lavaca Streets and Garfield Ally neighborhood circa 1963. The San Antonio skyline is as it looked just a couple years before HemisFair '68 came and changed it forever. A wide-angle lens pushed the tall buildings downtown farther away than they actually are, but it's still a lovely view of an old neighborhood. *Circa 1963, $4-5.*

Seen from about the same direction but higher up and later, this aerial shot features the modern, city-owned, high-rise apartment for seniors named Victoria Plaza. My grandmother lived there for a few years after retiring from many years as a nurse since it was and still is ideal for those on a fixed income. *Circa 1968, $2-4.*

From high atop the Tower of the Americas beats the new heart of the city situated along Alamo, Market and East Commerce Streets. The modularly built Hilton Palacia del Rio Hotel faces the Henry B. Gonzales Convention Center at the bottom. Both structures were built to capitalize on business and tourism expected from HemisFair 1968, the first officially designated world's fair held in the American southwest. St. Paul's Church sits nestled within the city block-sized Joskes Department Store while, far in the distance, Fredericksburg Road disappears into the northwest horizon. *Circa 1970, $3-5.*

Looking west on East Houston Street from Alamo Plaza this photographer caught the busy thoroughfare at noontime on a cloudless summer day after World War II. Block after block of retail shops, Five & Dime stores with lunch counters, eateries, a couple movie palaces, and other assorted businesses kept lively Houston Street busy from morning to night everyday of the week, especially on Saturdays. But never on Sundays. And this was before central air conditioning as shown by all the open windows in the Woolworth Co. on the left and the Gibbs Building on the right above the Sommers Drug Store. *Circa 1950, $6-8.*

Looking south across Alamo Plaza towards Saint Paul's Church, the then , red-brick Joskes Dept. Store sits at Commerce and Alamo streets a few years before WWI. In the foreground, peddlers and vendors move about the unpaved plaza in their horse carts and buckbords, adjacent to the Alamo's yet-to-be restored "Long Barracks" on the left. *Circa 1908, $4-6.*

Looking east past the Alameda Theater at 318 West Houston Street, this card offers the exact opposite view from the previous one and at about the same time. When it was built by local businessman Tano Lucchese in 1949, the Alameda was the largest facility in America dedicated exclusively to Spanish entertainment, movies, stage shows, and concerts. After years of neglect, the old venue has been restored as The Alameda National Center for Latino Arts and Culture and features the completely renovated 2,400-seat theater. *Circa 1950, $6-8*

Alamo Plaza has long been a downtown focal point as seen here looking north after 1900 when horse-drawn hacks lined up waiting for guests from the Menger Hotel. Way across the plaza sat San Antonio's tallest structure, the Maverick Building, and the fortress like Post Office on Houston Street. Among the trees sat the green helmeted bandstand that was later relocated to San Pedro Park, where it still exists today. *Circa 1908, $4-6.*

The Cenotaph today is solidly splendid as ever looming over the plaza. Created in 1939 from white marble on a pink granite base by famed Italian sculptor Pompeo Coppini, it is sixty feet tall and supposedly marks the place of cremation for the Alamo's defenders by order of Gen. Santa Ana. We know now that the bodies were burned elsewhere, that most likely was near the old Alameda east and south of the mission/fort along present day East Commerce Street.

The striking 1926 Medical Arts Building & Hospital towers over the Alamo circa 1956 judging by the cars parked in front of the old chapel. As a child with bad allergies, I visited a former army doctor there who injected everybody with a B-12 shot regardless of their complaint; including the doctor himself on a daily basis. It always hurt like hell, but he swore by them so it must have been a good thing. Dr. Moore's office windows were about where the Texas flag flies in this neat view. *Circa 1960, $2-3.*

This elevated 1950 view of Alamo Plaza looking northeast shows the main structures then as now to be the old Federal Building/Main Post Office. The tall Medical Arts tower looms over the Alamo grounds across Houston Street while looking up Avenue E one sees the old *Express-News* building where the city's main daily newspaper was and is published. Across Avenue E from the *Express-News* sits the monumental Scottish Rite Cathedral visible to the right of the Medical Arts Building here. *Circa 1950, $4-5. Courtesy of Craig Covner.*

A 1960s street-level view of Alamo Plaza featured the newer 1936 Federal building, Cenotaph monument for the Alamo's fallen heroes, and classic Gibbs building. Barely visible in front of the Cenotaph's flowers is a sun dial I used many times. I became good at telling time the old-fashion way. I received a nice watch as a high school graduation gift in May 1963, but lost it by year's end, so it was back to the sun dial whenever I was downtown. *Circa 1960, $2-4.*

HemisFair 1968 was the first officially designated international exposition in the American southwest. It ran from April 6 to October 6, 1968 with the theme being "Confluence of Civilizations in the Americas." It attracted more than 6.3 million visitors in those six months and the Tower continues to draw visitors from around the world and apparently outer space as well. *Circa 1968 $1-3.*

UFO NEAR TOWER OF THE AMERICAS

Below: I would not visit the Tower in its first few years because of an accident when the observation deck/gondola was first being raised. While being lifted, the large top section fell back down from about fifty feet up. As seen in this archival photo, following repairs, the large gondola was successfully raised to the top where it has since been visited by many thousands of visitors each year.

Above: From its opening in 1968 until 1996, HemisFair's 622 foot tall Tower of the Americas was the highest observation platform in the United States until surpassed by a Las Vegas structure. The HemisFair Tower offers spectacular vistas in all directions and is well worth the elevator ride for a look around or to dine in the tower's sky-high restaurant. *Circa 1990, $2-3.*

Hemisfair Plaza - San Antonio, Texas

Photo by Mac Miller

When Hemisfair 1968 opened, this was the main entrance on South Alamo Street. Visitors entered the fairgrounds through Hemisfair Plaza seen here. *Circa 1968 $2-4.*

A HemisFair mariachi band plays for an audience during the daily festivities. In the background a pair of the skyway cable cars pass each other while moving across the nearly 100-acre fairground. *Circa 1968, $1-3.*

The popular monorail moved Fair goers from point to point with an elevated view of the grounds. A few years after the fair closed it was still being operated when an unfortunate accident killed a rider when the car fell from the raised track. *Circa 1968, $1-3.*

This linen card shows San Antonio's first section of post- WW II modern expressway that opened in 1949. The view is northwest out what became I-10. A pink roadway was more likely the result of poor color coordination by the card printer than actual fact. *Circa 1950, $2-3.*

New Express Highway, San Antonio, Texas

Skyline of San Antonio, Texas

This late 1950s postcard shows the well-known fork in the city's growing expressway just northwest of downtown. The city skyline as of 1960 had changed a lot from the previous view of fifty years earlier. It would change much more dramatically by 2000 as even larger and taller buildings were erected. Above, at night that was a tricky fork in the freeway and, if you weren't paying attention, you went in the opposite direction. *Circa 1958, $2-3.*

One of San Antonio's most historic businesses was Joske's Department Stores, which began operating on Main Plaza in 1867. Relocating to Alamo and East Commerce Streets a few years later, Joske's opened their big store, seen here, in 1887. By 1910 it had grown to five floors with elevators and electric lights. *Circa 1910, $4-5.*

This is the well known Joske's facade after major additions and renovation were begun in 1936 and renewed again in the late 1940s. Modernization brought this distinctive limestone covering with nameplate and air-conditioning as a Texas first in large retail stores. Following more modifications taking it to five floors and 551,000 square feet by 1953, making it the largest department store west of the Mississippi, Joske's was known as "the biggest store in the biggest state." By then it surrounded St. Paul's Church and covered two full city blocks. The little church soon became known as "Saint Joskes." *Circa 1960, $5-8.*

Standing at East Commerce and Alamo Streets this clever photographer pointed his camera north toward Alamo Plaza around 1910. On the right is Joskes and across the street is Sol Wolfson's Store in the 1883 Dullnig Building. *Circa 1910, $4-7.*

On Saturdays and during the Christmas season "Big Mo" carried shoppers to and from their cars throughout the huge parking lot that covered another couple city blocks. Throughout the 1950s and '60s the famous downtown flagship store was the busiest retailer in South Texas, frequently drawing shoppers from Mexico. Historic Joske's closed its doors in 1987 after having changed ownership of its 27-store chain; it is now a Dillard's Department Store. *Circa 1961, $8-10.*

San Antonio's first public library was this Andrew Carnegie funded one built in 1911 at Market and South Presa Streets. It was replaced in 1938 by a more modern building that served until 1968. *Circa 1924, $2-3.*

This nearly windowless building became the Central Library in 1968 at 131 South Main Street. It served the city until a more artistic design was selected. *Circa 1970, $2-4.*

Carnegie Public Library, San Antonio, Texas.

"Winter Playground of America."

A simple block built edifice was the city's second main public library seen here. It was built on the same site as its predecessor at 210 Market St. backed up to the River Walk. This card robs the beautiful old building of all its ornate sculpture and artwork. Bas-reliefs of Cervantes and Shakespeare grace either side of the arched entryway as well as other surprises if you look. Above the front door are these important words: "Next In Importance To Freedom And Justice Is Popular Education Without Which Neither Freedom Nor Justice Can Be Permanently Maintained." *Circa 1930, $3-4.*

North on San Pedro sits San Antonio College where I began my quest for higher education in 1963. SAC moved here in 1951 and is the largest single-campus community college in Texas with a student body of over 20,000. The dome above the campus is not SAC's famous planetarium, but the Temple Beth-El Synagogue. *Circa 1955, $3-5.*

Today's Central Library is a striking Mexican Modernist design nicknamed "the Red Enchilada" because of its eye catching color. Costing $28 million dollars it opened in 1995 at 600 Soledad and quickly became very popular for its artfulness inside and out.

Shown in the bottom right corner is the old Sears & Roebuck store at the intersection of Soledad and Navarro Streets where "the Red Enchilada" library now stands. Across the street is the Baptist Medical Center where I was born a long time ago in the older building near the middle of the photo. *Circa 1970, $3-4.*

San Antonio. Texas. Avenue C. Hotel.

Avenue C Hotel

The Avenue C Hotel, located on San Antonio's Broadway—Avenue C and Fifth Street, is one of the most select Family Hotels and affords its patrons the full enjoyment of the excellent climate of the Alamo City by the use of its 750 feet running galleries around the building.

26488©

The Avenue C Hotel was a popular turn-of-the-century stop for traveling families and ordinary vacationers. They preferred the downtown environs to that offered by the railroad depot situated hotels intended mainly for traveling salesman. Circa 1910, $5-8. **Courtesy of Norman Porter**.

Chapter Four:
It Pays to Advertise

A category of postcards not necessarily aimed only at tourists but at everyone was those published strictly as commercial advertising. Locally owned print shops and large postcard companies once had salesmen making calls encouraging businesses of all sizes, shapes, and locations to invest in postcards as a way of advertising their place, product, or service. Perhaps most common in this category are those offered by hotels, restaurants, and retailers of all kinds to their customers past, present, and future. And, once again, thanks to the convenience and availability of the Real Photo Post Card, many small businessmen could produce smaller batches of cards to give away or sell. Anyone with a good camera could take a fair photograph of his own or a friend's business and then order any number of RPPC-type prints from the photo processor. This leaves us with a partial record of stores, shops, and businesses that might otherwise have been long ago forgotten just as it has left records of events or happenings not formally recorded.

WESTERN SUN MOTEL

Fifty years later, by 1960, places like the Western Sun Motel on Austin Highway catered to families traveling by car rather than trains. Before the interstate highways were built old main roads like U.S. 81, here known as Austin Highway were filled with motels and some remain in business. *Circa 1963, $3-5.*

Pearl Brewery San Antonio Tex. 7/3/09

Part of San Antonio's historic German heritage was the large-scale production of beer over the years. Built just northeast of downtown in 1894 by the San Antonio Brewing Association, this landmark brewery was home to Pearl Beer for 115 years. *RPPC Dated 7-3-1909, $9-15.*

The same brewery sixty years later had grown in size and stature, as Pearl Beer was sold statewide until this historic site closed in 2001. *Circa 1969, $5-7.*

Another advertising card from Pearl Brewing Co., this one was a humorous attempt to teach Pearl Beer drinkers a little German while they enjoyed the brew. *Circa 1964, $2-3.*

Fall 2007 saw the old brewery being restored in phases by Silver Ventures, a San Antonio-based investment firm. The plans call for an events hall, schools, mixed retail and office space plus some upscale residential space.

The original Lone Star Brewery here on Jones Avenue just off Broadway was producing 65,000 barrels of beer annually by 1903. That ended with Prohibition then it sat empty for many years until 1981 when the old building reopened as the San Antonio Museum of Art.

Lone Star, "The National Beer of Texas," had changed hands a few times when the brewery finally closed in 1998. The beer is produced elsewhere now, but the old plant is slowly being allowed to wither on the vine as seen in this October 2007 shot.

Across town just off Roosevelt Avenue was Lone Star Brewing Company, Pearl's main local competitor for decades. The first LSB brewery was built in 1904 just north of downtown; this modern plant opened in 1934. A pecan tree shaded park and picnic ground with this large swimming pool was available to employees for family parties or cookouts. *Circa 1964, $5-7.*

The historic, large scale production of beer in this city required equal amounts of block ice to keep it cold and thus was born the "ice house" in the 1920s. They were built all over town and became part convenience store, part tavern, or a place to just hang out. Right: Neighborhood Ice operated for many years at South Gevers Avenue and Highland Boulevard. In the good old days, you drove up and a guy came to your car, you ordered a cold Lone Star long neck and some tamales or a Big Red Soda and potato chips and were on your way in a minute or two. Now that's what I call convenience. *Circa 1986, $8-10.*

Soft drinks were also popular beverages as this nice ad-card from the Dragon Bottling Company documented. This small label probably sold mostly in San Antonio and surrounding towns when such production was more local. The name suggests that it had caffeine like many modern so-called "power drinks" do now. *Circa 1947, $5-7.*

This Humble Oil Company trailer-tanker sits at the company terminal on El Paso Street strung with garlands for the 1930 Battle of Flowers Parade. With hands on his hips, the driver was my grandfather Mr. C. K. Brown who drove mule teams and then trucks for Humble for thirty-four years. *RPPC, Dated August 1938, $8-10.*

Across the street from the Humble station was a large area of city cemeteries that stretched for several blocks along New Braunfels Avenue. Near my dad's place was this huge city water tank. It was erected about 1920 just outside the Hermann Sons Cemetery and stood there for nearly sixty years adjacent to Saint Gerards High School. The tall cylindrical tank was an old familiar neighborhood landmark so somebody made an RPPC postcard of it. *Dated March 3, 1946, $8-10.*

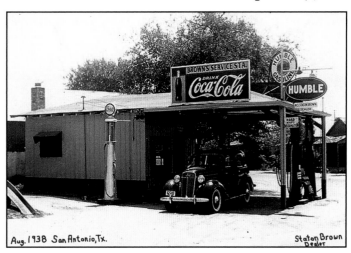

An August 1938 view of Brown's Service Station shows a customer's sedan under the Coca-Cola sign. The station was directly across the street from a large cemetery so it got little business at night. It closed when World War II began. *Dated August 1938. Courtesy of Bob Brown.*

My dad's Humble station was at 210 South New Braunfels Avenue for a couple of years following his graduation from high school. This small frame building was torn down after World War II and a larger modern station was built, which lasted into the 1970s. *Dated August 1938, $8-10. Courtesy of Bob Brown.*

48

Mike Persia Chevrolet, originally from New Orleans, had dealers in several southern cities including Houston and San Antonio. This one opened in the mid 1950s at Saint Mary's and East Nueva Streets just south of the Plaza Hotel. Its catchy jingle and TV ads made it a well-known business for many years in the area. *Circa 1964, $4-6.*

ACE Supply Company was another locally owned business that invested in full color Kodachrome type postcards to enhance its reputation. Their 1959 Chevrolet El Camino with mini-trailer sits ready to deliver plumbing supplies anywhere in town. *Circa 1960, $2-4.*

Another local business for many years was van Hardeveld's Uniform Center at 206 Broadway. Mr. van Hardeveld was proud enough of his products and shop to procure a batch of handsome chromo graphic postcards. *Circa 1960, $5-6.*

Since 1929, Riverside Municipal Golf Course has provided a moderately challenging course of play for "duffers" and pros as its 18 holes sprawl along the historic San Antonio River south of town. For many years, the Golf Motel sat at 1711 Roosevelt Avenue on the north end of the public course, glimpsed beyond the motel fence in the lower half of this advertising card. Beginning about the time these photos were taken, I caddied there for my dad who was an award-winning golfer. Perhaps of more historical importance is the fact that in 1898, Col. Teddy Roosevelt drilled his legendary horse cavalry known as the "Rough Riders" in the open pastures that later became Riverside Golf Course. *Circa 1958, $4-5.*

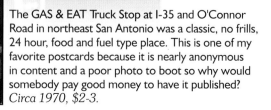

The GAS & EAT Truck Stop at I-35 and O'Connor Road in northeast San Antonio was a classic, no frills, 24 hour, food and fuel type place. This is one of my favorite postcards because it is nearly anonymous in content and a poor photo to boot so why would somebody pay good money to have it published? *Circa 1970, $2-3.*

The Magnolia Filling Station sits at the fork of Broadway and Austin Highway in Alamo Heights. It opened in 1934 and after many years of pumping gasoline, closed. It then sat empty for many more years and is now a realtor's offices.

DAMONS Fine Foods was located at 110 Austin Highway next to the landmark Magnolia Filling Station. That restaurant was a joint venture of Damon, George, and William Tassos that later became the well-remembered Bean Pot owned solely by Wallace Tassos. Famous for his signature baked beans, it operated for nearly twenty years before closing in 1980. The property was bought by Frost Bank, which tore it down in the mid 1990s to erect a bank.
Circa 1965, $2-3.

The much-loved EARL ABEL'S Restaurant sat at Broadway and Hildebrand Streets for over sixty-five years. Begun in 1940 as a drive-up hamburger stand and soda fountain with carhops, the popular location evolved into a full service sit down restaurant. *Circa 1980, $3-5.*

In 2006, the long favored EARL ABEL'S eatery was demolished to make way for more modern development. New owners then opened a reborn EARL ABEL'S Restaurant at 1201 Austin Highway in the long-standing Terrell Plaza Shopping Center. *Courtesy of Bob Brown.*

La Fonda is San Antonio's oldest Mexican Restaurant. It's been in business since 1936 at 2415 North Main Avenue in the historic Monte Vista neighborhood. *Circa 1970, $2-3*

The city's oldest steak house is The Barn Door Restaurant at 8400 North New Braunfels Street. It opened in 1953 at the site of an old stagecoach agency located on the historic Camino Real or King's Highway. *Circa 1955, $2-3.*

Still offering their popular "mesquite grilled meats," the Barn Door continues to feed hungry guests and operate a retail meat market at 8400 North New Braunfels Street in Alamo Heights near Loop 410. *Circa 2007, $2-3. Courtesy of Bob Brown.*

For many years at 400 East Josephine Street near the old Pearl Brewery was E. J. Fincke's Meat Market & Grocery. Mom & pop meat market/groceries like this one once dotted the city's many neighborhoods in the days before supermarkets. This one at Josephine and Avenue A was probably typical in many ways. *Circa 1940, $9-14.*

Derelict for many years, the small building was bought, remodeled, and opened in 1979 as the Josephine Street Cafe, home to good Steaks and Whiskey as the neon-lit windows advertise.

Across Avenue A from Fincke's is the Liberty Schooner Saloon that was opened in 1890 by Fritz Boehler, a Pearl Beer brew master. The infamous 1921 flood gave this place its famous tilt while it is the oldest continually operating saloon in San Antonio. It later became Boehler's Beer Garden, and as a 17-year-old college freshman, I enjoyed the homemade beef stew and a schooner of beer here at lunchtime, no ID required.

54

A few blocks away back at 1507 Broadway stands another old time San Antonio icon, The Pig Stand (# 29). This drive-in eatery has been here since 1930, as seen in this vintage RPPC, offering America's "Motor Lunch" as provided by uniformed carhops. *RPPC, circa 1940, $20-25. Courtesy of Hailey Family via TxDoT.*

Today the old Pig Stand is still there and serving classic Texas comfort foods like chicken-fried steak, enchiladas, catfish, hamburgers, and of course their trademark BBQ Pork Sandwich. No more car hops but it's worth walking into and sitting down to be served. They occasionally host classic car clubs that show up in their restored Chevys, Fords, and other serious hotrods of years past. *Circa 2007, $2-3. Courtesy of Bob Brown.*

Long gone and surely forgotten is the "No Name Cafe and Restaurant" at 640 East Commerce Street, "Near S. P. Depot, P. W. Schliesling, Prop." This great view comes on an early "colorized" postcard typical of the first decade of the twentieth century. A smart businessman might have given this card away as a means of spreading the word about his eatery. *Circa 1907, $6-10.*

Over at 450 Fredericksburg Road was LEO'S, 24-hour
"Home to the world's tastiest BAR-B-CUED RIBS." Leo also
offered hungry San Antonians breakfast, lunch, and dinner.
Circa 1950, $4-6.

Further out Fredericksburg Road, the
KIT KAT KLUB was one of the city's hottest nightclubs
for many years. Famous for its "Barbecue Bar" and "Champaign
Cocktails" this upscale nightclub had live big band dance music and
fine dining for the more affluent patrons in town. *Circa 1946, $7-10.*

Downtown at 424 East Commerce Street is San Antonio's oldest and one of its best restaurants, Schilo's Delicatessen (pronounced She-lows). Serving fine German style brats, sandwiches, soups and such since 1917, this place is the real deal. It has changed very little in the past fifty-six years since my grandfather first took me in there at age five. We always had a bowl of their wonderful split pea soup, Jewish rye bread with butter and a frosted mug of their homemade root beer. *Circa 2007, $2-3.*

Three generations enjoyed Schilo's root beer and split pea soup as my son Leland, my grandfather C. K. Brown, and I sat there at the bar in December 1979. Walk in today and it looks mostly the same and they are still serving the same great foods. As soon as one enters, Schilo's is instantly recognizable by its smell, which hasn't changed in the fifty-six years since I first walked in. That's a good thing.

Chapter Five:
Special Places

All over San Antonio there are to be found a number of special places. Some are gone and some remain that are still truly unique. We have cards for some of these places beginning with sports venues, a zoo, and amusement parks. Some are gone now, but the memories persist through postcards that help us recall the better days. Like most American cities, this one has always supported sports teams from the high school and college variety to professional ones. Baseball was historically the most popular, but never enough so for a national level team. There were also a few unsuccessful attempts to bring professional football to the city. Then something sort of unique happened and since 1973 San Antonio has been home to one of the most winning professional basketball teams in America, the SPURS of NBA fame. They now have their own major facility built by AT&T.

San Antonio's Zoo is like most other zoos except that it was built into the same old limestone quarry from where the stone came to build the Alamo and other historic structures in town. Next to the Zoo is the truly unique Sunken Gardens with an unusual history of its own. The old cement plant was reborn as a home to a special family, but there were both bright and dark years due to World War II. Both locations are part of the larger Brackenridge Park that has seen many changes over the years and is still a popular family gathering place.

Old movie venues are among the most sought after images on postcards especially driven-ins, and San Antonio had nearly two dozen of them once upon a time but no more. It also had many small neighborhood movie houses, but none survived as such. One special old movie theater remains open—but not for movies anymore.

After a number of team affiliations and name changes, the San Antonio Missions were back in town as of 1988 playing in a borrowed facility. In 1994 this park was built as the Nelson W. Wolff Municipal Stadium, named for a former mayor who was also a minor league baseball player in his youth. *Courtesy of Eric and Wendy Pastore.*

MISSION STADIUM stood on the city's south side at Mitchell and Mission Roads from 1947 to 1974. It was home to the San Antonio Missions, a Texas League farm team of the St. Louis Browns. *Circa 1956, $9-15.*

58

Brooks Robinson

3rd BASE BALTIMORE ORIOLES

The
back of his Topps
"rookie baseball card" referred to his
play at San Antonio. Other famous Texas leaguers who
played at San Antonio are Dizzy Dean, Dennis Eckersley, Orel Hershiser,
Joe Morgan, Fernando Valenzuela, Paul Konerko, and Mike Piazza.

In 1956, future Hall of Fame player Brooks
Robinson was a 19-year-old rookie third
baseman for the San Antonio Missions. That
year the Missions were a St. Louis Browns
minor league team that later became the
Baltimore Orioles.

BROOKS IS A YOUNG
PROSPECT FOR FUTURE
STARDOM

Height: 6'1"
Weight: 180
Bats: Right
Throws: Right
Home:
Little Rock,
Ark.
Born:
May 18, 1937

"Bush league" teams were always
around town somewhere and
this RPPC shows the San Antonio
Black Sox Champions for 1950.
They were part of the old South
Texas Negro League that began in
1945 and lasted until 1980. This
image was shot at old Pittman
Sullivan Park near Saint Gerards
High School on New Braunfels
Avenue on the city's East Side.
The tall water tank seen in
another RPPC card is on the hill
behind the team. *Dated 1950,
$8-10.*

8 - Alamo Stadium, San Antonio, Texas

Since opening in 1940, the 23,000 seat Alamo Stadium has long been home to many of the city's older high schools and often sells out for the notorious "Annual Chili Bowl Game." This contest pits Fox Tech and Lanier High Schools, two inner city, largely Hispanic institutions each year. It has also hosted many college and professional football games as well. *Circa 1940, $2-3.*

Looking like a cross between a space station and a futuristic riverboat is the Alamo Dome, which opened in 1993 amid much controversy and scandal. Originally built for the San Antonio SPURS pro basketball team it now has no professional sports affiliation. *Circa 2006, $1.*

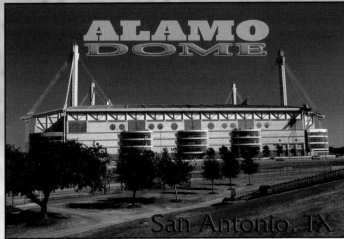

ALAMO DOME

San Antonio, TX

JOE FREEMAN COLISEUM
San Antonio, Texas

Since opening in 1949 the Joe Freeman Coliseum in far east San Antonio has hosted an amazing variety of events, festivals, performances, fairs, and concerts. Most historically significant of all these has been the annual San Antonio Stock Show & Rodeo which began at the Coliseum in 1950. Perhaps its quirkiest but historic show was the 1966 appearance of a relatively unknown British rock & roll band named the Rolling Stones. *Circa 1960, $2-3.*

Now named the AT&T Center, this futuristic structure was built as the new home for the San Antonio SPURS basketball team. It was completed in 2002 at a cost of $175 million and seats 18,500 for the SPURS home games, 13,000 for hockey and 19,000 for concerts or religious events, plus fifty luxury suites for private corporate parties. The modern facility is also home to the San Antonio Silver Stars (WNBA) and the San Antonio Rampage (AHL); it is located adjacent to the Joe Freeman Coliseum on East Houston Street. *Circa 2006, $2-3.*

60

In 1899 former Austinite George Brackenridge donated nearly two hundred acres to the city for a park to be created along the northern part of the San Antonio River. By 1940 Brackenridge Park had a zoo, golf course, swimming beach, polo field and Alligator Garden seen here. It had live "alligator wrestling" and exhibits plus souvenirs. It has been closed and empty since the early 1950s. *Circa 1955, $3-5.*

The large park's most well known attraction has long been the San Antonio Zoological Gardens established in 1914 within an old limestone quarry. That natural walled barrier was ready made for housing animals and in November 1929, two of the first cage-less exhibits in America, the Barless Bear Terraces and the Primate Paradise, were opened. The "Bear Pit" gave visitors a look at bears moving about nearly naturally rather than being confined in cages. *Circa 1940, $2-3.*

BEAR PIT IN BRACKENRIDGE PARK, SAN ANTONIO, TEXAS—59

MONKEY ISLAND, BRECKENRIDGE PARK, SAN ANTONIO, TEXAS

The Primate paradise or "Monkey Island" was also popular for watching families of monkeys interacting in a semi-natural setting. *Circa 1940, $2-3.*

This early postcard suggests that it was once possible to drive through the Zoo while viewing the animals. The high quarry wall can be seen rising behind the animal compounds. *Circa 1925, $6-8. Courtesy of Ned Coleman.*

21:—ZOO, BRACKENRIDGE PARK, SAN ANTONIO, TEXAS

An adolescent hippo gets a treat from a careful attendant. In the Zoo today are over 3,500 animals representing 750 species held within fifty-six acres of modern enclosures. *Circa 1968, $2-3.*

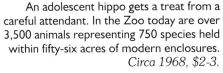

Welcome to the
San Antonio Zoo

The San Antonio Zoo is still pulling families, tourists, and locals into the unique limestone environment that has been its home for nearly a century. More than 850,000 guests visit the San Antonio Zoo each year and nearly a quarter of them are children coming on school field trips. *Circa 2007, $1-2.*

Sunken Garden in Brackenridge Park

Photo by Mac Miller

Cement Plant, Brackenridge Park, San Antonio, Texas

Brackenridge Park's most unique feature is the Japanese Sunken Gardens and Tea House. Begun in 1917 in the abandoned limestone quarry next to the Zoo, these beautiful lily ponds and walkways have a dark chapter in their history. That story was inadvertently recorded on postcards published during World War II. *Circa 1983, $2-3.*

The Sunken Garden's historic kiln and cottages remain from the quarry era when it manufactured Portland cement. This old chimney sits atop the kilns used to produce quicklime for cement. The limestone itself was being quarried and used to construct the state capitol in Austin and buildings in downtown San Antonio. *Circa 1965, $3-4.*

A local Japanese immigrant, artist Kimi Eizo Jingu, and his wife Miyoshi were hired by the city to live in and manage the Tea House cafe beginning in 1926. This hand built, stone and thatched pavilion covered the tables and chairs used by the cafe's customers. *Circa 1968, $3-4.*

This gate to the Gardens was made by famed Mexican artisan Dionicio Rodriguez before World War II when it was known as the Japanese Sunken Gardens. Kimi passed away in 1936, but Miyoshi and their eight children lived in the Gardens until Japanese naval air forces attacked Pearl Harbor in December 1941. The family was then evicted and the name was changed to Chinese Sunken Gardens. *Circa 1965, $2-3.*

In this prewar postcard, daughter Mary Jingu is standing on a garden path in her traditional Japanese kimono with a proper title above the image. To the uninformed this lovely linen post card provides an exotic scene direct from Japan. *Circa 1940, $3-4.*

A couple of years later during World War II, the name has been changed to Chinese Sunken Gardens with Mary Jingu still there but supposedly now a Chinese girl. *Circa 1942, $3-4.*

Here is the exact same scene minus Mary in her kimono and oddly, a typo in the title. Now it is shown as being wrongly at Breckenridge Park but the scene was politically correct. Mary's brother James was wounded and decorated later in the war while serving in France with the legendary, all Japanese American 442nd Regimental Combat Team. *Circa 1944, $3-4*
As a footnote, in 1984 surviving members of the Jingu family returned to San Antonio for a ceremony at the Gardens hosted by Mayor Henry Cisneros. The Jingu family was recognized for its sacrifices during the war and the original name of Japanese Tea House and Sunken Gardens was restored to the popular site.

This 2006 view of the Sunken Gardens shows it overgrown with no water in the pools, no koi, flowers, or people as it was closed to the public. Friends of the Parks is a local volunteer group dedicated to raise funds for restoring Sunken Gardens to its original condition before reopening this magical place to the public as soon as possible.

Another popular feature of the large park is the two-mile long Brackenridge Eagle Miniature Train that travels through the 343 acre park daily and crosses the San Antonio River twice. The Eagle celebrated its first fifty years of service in 2007 and has been robbed only once. *Circa 1970, $5-7.*

While carrying nearly eighty passengers, in July 1977 the Eagle was stopped by two robbers in a wooded area near Witte Museum. The men got away with a few hundred dollars, a couple credit cards, a camera, and some cotton candy. The two youthful bandits were later apprehended and sent to prison as the city takes a dim view of tourists being robbed while vacationing here. *Circa 1970, $5-7.*

Another popular place near Brackenridge Park was the old Playland at North Alamo and Broadway Streets. Opened in 1940 it was home to the truly scary Rocket Roller Coaster and many other classic thrill rides until closing in 1980. This linen from the late 1940s is apparently the only postcard that Playland ever printed. The Rocket went to Knoebels Amusement Park in Elysburg, Pennsylvania and was renamed The Phoenix. *Circa 1950, $-5-7.*

Kids enjoyed the famous 1917 C. W. Parker built Carousel also found at Playland from 1940 to 1980. Parker named his rides "Carry-Us-Alls" rather than Merry-Go-Round and this one was a beauty. Sadly when the park closed it was auctioned off piece-by-piece, horse-by-horse. *Circa 1979, $3-5.*

The city now owns the long abandoned Playland Park acreage with uncertain plans for its future. An historic irrigation ditch of the Acequia Madre de Valero dating from the Spanish Colonial period runs through the grounds.

A few blocks north on Broadway Street is a scaled down, kids-only amusement venue named "Kiddie Park" that opened in 1925 well before its long abandoned counterpart. It is still thrilling small children with a modest collection of antique attractions including the Little Dipper Roller Coaster, a toddler sized Ferris Wheel and a beautiful Carousel built in 1918 plus several other pint sized rides. *Circa 2007, $2-3.*

This early 1980s Kodachrome card shows the 1918 Herschell-Spillman Carousel placed in the park in 1935. It was built as a "carnival model" intended to be moved frequently from town to town, but has operated at 3015 Broadway for over seventy years. *Circa 1980, $3-5.*

Kiddie Park's charm comes from the simplicity of its old and worn rides as seen in this 1980 Kodachrome card. I can remember going there as a kid and taking my own kids there thirty years later. On weekends the acre-sized park is full of parents and children usually celebrating a birthday party. *Circa 1980, $3-5.*

Hot Well's Hotel, San Antonio, Tex.

Across town, on South Presa Street, the almost mythical Hot Wells Hotel remains abandoned but not forgotten. Once San Antonio's premier spa and resort for the idle rich and famous, it was the subject of many colorful postcards during its heyday and its long history is also well documented. The 1906 Cincinnati Reds baseball team held their spring training camp here and enjoyed the waters. *Circa 1907, $6-8.*

Corner of Lobby of Hot Wells Hotel, San Antonio, Texas.

This lobby view shows the rattan furniture, ceiling fans, and electric lights at Hot Wells during its prime. Sadly, all this was lost to a terrible fire in 1925. After World War II new owners turned the old Bath Pavilion into a restaurant/bar named the Flame Room. *Circa 1906, $4-6.*

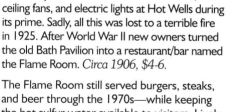

The Flame Room still served burgers, steaks, and beer through the 1970s—while keeping the hot sulfur water available to visitors. Lively New Year's Eve parties ended an era; in 1974 since upkeep was never a priority, there was another fire and in 1988 yet another fire gutted the old building. Crumbling remains are the only reminder of a once bustling resort. *Courtesy of Greg Eckhardt.*

Pool, Hot Wells Bath House, San Antonio, Texas.

Shown are the indoor pools that made Hot Wells so popular for their supposed curative powers. Many celebrities of the era traveled to Hot Wells including President Theodore Roosevelt, humorist/actor Will Rogers, filmmaker comedian Charlie Chaplin, silent movie cowboy star Tom Mix, and legendary film director Cecil B. De Mille. *Circa 1910, $5-7.*

Bathing Pavilion, Hot Wells Hotel, San Antonio, Texas.

The Hot Wells Bathing Pavilion housed the geothermal pools that people came to experience for the curative powers. Naturally heated spring water smelled strongly of sulfur but most visitors were willing to endure it in exchange for the healthy effects of bathing there. This is the bath building that survived well into the 1980s when a fire left it in ruins. *Circa 1920, $6-8.*

HOT WELLS LODGES
5503 S. Presa Street
SAN ANTONIO, TEXAS

A fire in 1925 destroyed the original hotel structure and by World War II new owners had transformed the property into a large trailer park named Hot Wells Lodges as seen in this aerial view. A restaurant/bar named the Flame Room was opened in the old Bath Pavilion that drew business from campers and from nearby Brooks Field. This card also shows the San Antonio River flowing along behind the old resort. *Circa 1944, $5-7.*

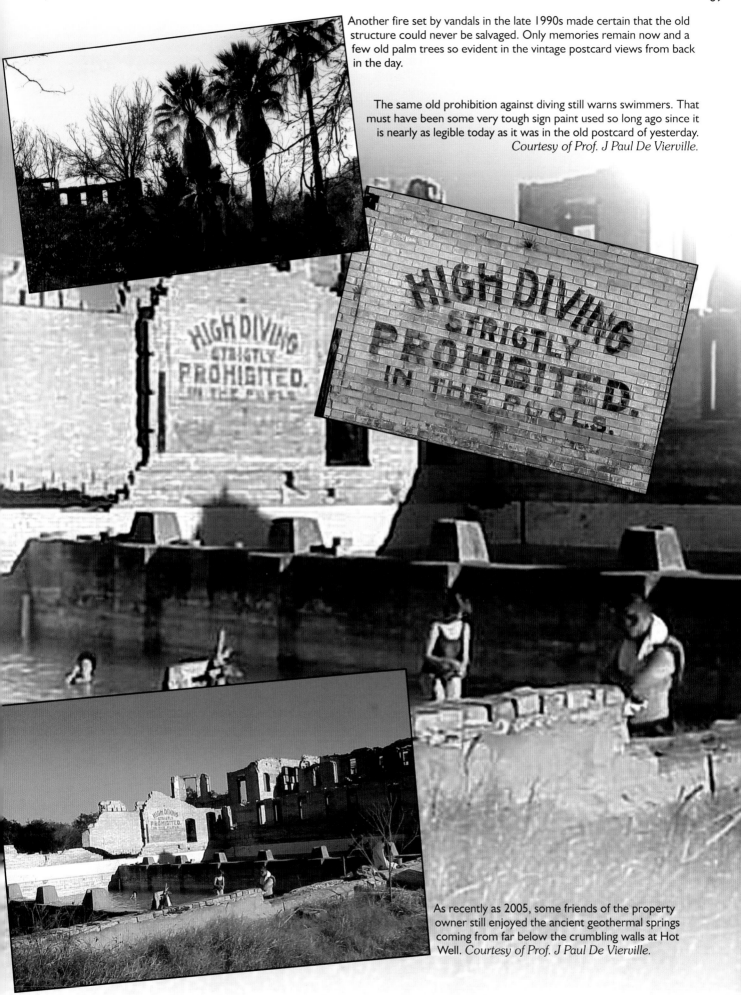

Another fire set by vandals in the late 1990s made certain that the old structure could never be salvaged. Only memories remain now and a few old palm trees so evident in the vintage postcard views from back in the day.

The same old prohibition against diving still warns swimmers. That must have been some very tough sign paint used so long ago since it is nearly as legible today as it was in the old postcard of yesterday. *Courtesy of Prof. J Paul De Vierville.*

As recently as 2005, some friends of the property owner still enjoyed the ancient geothermal springs coming from far below the crumbling walls at Hot Well. *Courtesy of Prof. J Paul De Vierville.*

Back in the day, visitors to Hot Wells used this little suspension bridge to cross the close-by San Antonio River as it meandered southward out of town. Usually it was crossed in order to tour the crumbling but historic walls of Mission San Jose a half mile away. In January of 1910 a film company moved onto a twenty-acre spread just over this bridge from Hot Wells and began making movies. *Circa 1912, $6-8.*

STAR Film Ranch headquartered in this large ranch house beginning in January 1910 as French filmmaker Gaston Melies escaped the cold winters of New York City. STAR Film Ranch made over seventy movies while in San Antonio, most of them western action stories with lots of cowboys, Indians, bandits, and damsels in distress, etc. *Circa 1910, $30-40. Courtesy of Frank Thompson.*

Left Column: *The Immortal Alamo No. 1 Lieutenant Dickenson is sent with a plea for aide to Gen. Sam Houston." Circa 1911, $90-100. Courtesy of Frank Thompson. The Immortal Alamo No. 2 shows Mexican army troops approaching the Alamo. Large groups of Mexican soldiers were portrayed by cadets from the local Peacock Military Academy. Circa 1911, $90-100. Courtesy of Frank Thompson. The Immortal Alamo No. 3 offers a good look at one of STAR Film's biggest stars, Miss Edith Storey, tending to a wounded "Col. Travis." Sets were built without roofs to let as much daylight in as possible for the early cameras and film. Circa 1911, $90-100. Courtesy of Frank Thompson.*

Right Column: *The Immortal Alamo No. 4 depicts the legendary battle's end at the Alamo chapel's entrance. The mission front was actually a cleverly painted backdrop with doors. Circa 1911, $90-100. Courtesy of Frank Thompson. The Immortal Alamo No. 5 was revisionist film making since Lt. Dickenson died at the Alamo. Circa 1911, $90-100. Courtesy of Frank Thompson. The Immortal Alamo No. 6 jumped ahead to the Battle of San Jacinto and Santa Anna's surrender to Gen. Sam Houston a month following the Alamo's fall. Circa 1911, $90-100. Courtesy of Frank Thompson.*

Another forgotten filmmaker from San Antonio's past was Spencer Williams whose 1946 movie "Beale Street Mama" was filmed here. Williams wrote and directed a number of films for the local Sack Amusement Company, which produced all black movies at a time when theaters were segregated. A night club scene was filmed in San Antonio bandleader Don Albert's Keyhole Club located at Pine and Iowa Streets on the city's East Side as seen in this miniature lobby card. The Key Hole opened in 1942 making it the first and only racially integrated venue in the South twenty years before the Civil Rights Act of 1964 that outlawed segregation. Playing in the movie's band was twenty-year-old tenor saxophonist "Zoot" Sims, then stationed at nearby Fort Sam Houston. The historic Army post was less than ten minutes away from the Key Hole so Sims, a former Benny Goodman bandsman, became a regular at the Sunday afternoon jam sessions in the club. *Circa 1946, $8-10.*

"Beale Street Mama" premiered in late 1946 at San Antonio's all black Cameo Theater that opened in 1940 at 1123 East Commerce Street. Until then black movie audiences were forced to attend movies at midnight screenings in downtown theaters like the Majestic or Aztec. Or they could watch earlier screenings from impossibly high balconies accessed through separate entrances at the rear of the Majestic and other movie houses. *Circa 1941 $8-10. RPPC courtesy of the Cameo Theater.*

The Cameo was an historic venue, but one with a relatively short career since black movie patrons could openly enter downtown theaters by the mid 1960s. It has been restored and as the CAMEO Center, it now regularly hosts live acts, plays, and bands on its stage. *Courtesy of Bob Brown.*

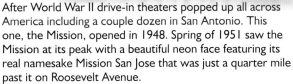

After World War II drive-in theaters popped up all across America including a couple dozen in San Antonio. This one, the Mission, opened in 1948. Spring of 1951 saw the Mission at its peak with a beautiful neon face featuring its real namesake Mission San Jose that was just a quarter mile past it on Roosevelt Avenue.

The Mission Drive-In Theater out lasted all the others in town; it finally closed for good in 2005, having lost its neon sign many years earlier. Three extra screens were added in the early 1960s, which helped it stay alive longer than the others, but eventually patrons stopped going in sufficient numbers and operating costs rose too high.

A mile beyond the Mission, where Roosevelt crossed Loop 13, sat the TRAIL Drive-In. It too had an eye-catching neon face that drew people in for many years finally closing like all the rest by the early 1980s. But this ad card is a nice reminder of the 1950s and '60s when families actually sat in their cars together for a few hours a night watching movies. *Circa 1973, $9-12.*

A Cavalier's River Parade 2007 float featuring Brooks City Base Fiesta Ambassadors moves along the beginning of the route. Behind the parade activity looms the old Milam Building still standing tall since 1928. *Circa 2007. Courtesy of the U.S. Air Force.*

Chapter Six:
"Remember the Alamo"

This well known and historic phrase may as well be San Antonio's official motto as the city has been remembering for over a hundred years both formally and casually in many ways. Each April for the annual observation of the Battle of San Jacinto or Texas Independence Day, San Antonio throws a weeklong party known as Fiesta. It is somewhat like Mardi Gras in New Orleans, but with three parades rather than only one. It begins with a water borne, River Walk float parade followed by fiestas every night that week. The big Battle of Flowers Parade happens downtown Friday afternoon with more fiestas and then closes with the unique Saturday night Flambeau Parade featuring illuminated floats and hundreds of torch-bearing marchers along the parade route.

The Alamo itself has long been at the very heart of San Antonio's image and character as the cradle of Texas independence. The impact that it has had and continues to have on the city is almost incalculable as is its importance to the Texas mythos in general. To many collectors, images of the Alamo have a nearly mystical quality and influence about them, so here are a number of rare or unusual ones. Books have been written on the changing appearance of the old "shrine" just as there have been arguments and controversies about how best to maintain its face and legacy. The physical structure is owned by the State of Texas and maintained and operated by the Daughters of the Texas Republic. This is an organization that actively perpetuates the memory of Texas pioneer families and soldiers of the Republic of Texas. Beyond that the Alamo is there for all who want to study its history, paint its portrait, write a song about it, make a movie depicting its fall, or any one of a countless number of ways in which to acknowledge its great legacy and presence as a national treasure. It is one of the most visited places in the world averaging 2.5 millions visitors a year.

Every year in April, Alamo City officials throw a ten-day long party now called Fiesta San Antonio, which began in 1891 as an observation of the victorious Battle of San Jacinto. Renowned San Antonio architect Atlee B. Ayers served as the Fiesta Association's first president from 1911 to 1918. This RPPC card shows him and his wife being honored in the 1956 night time Flambeau Parade. *Circa 1956, $10-15. Courtesy of Fernando Cortez.*

Atlee B. Ayers 1st President, Fiesta San Jacinto Assoc.

Fiesta Monday features the nighttime Texas Cavaliers River Parade as thousands of people line the entire River Walk through downtown. They come to see the newly crowned King of Fiesta take his seat to watch the watery parade. The Cavalier king is in a turquoise cap and jacket with red trousers near the left edge of the scene. *Circa 1955, $3-5.*

This rare RPPC shows the All Nations portion of the Battle of Flowers Parade. Mexico was represented with a float led by vaqueros (cowboys) riding north on Alamo Street toward Houston Street and the Post Office. They were passing the Palace Theater and were nearly to Woolworth's when photographed. *Dated April 20 1927, $9-14. Courtesy of Norman Porter.*

Each year huge crowds in excess of 300,00 spectators line downtown sidewalks to watch area high school bands and ROTC units, military bands and formations, and colorful floats pass along the streets all afternoon. Here the Queen's Float heralds the parade's final section as it passes the Majestic Theater on Houston Street. *Circa 1965, $5-7.*

A big part of the annual Fiesta Parade are the area's many high school bands. This is the Robert E. Lee H.S. Band of 1969 under the direction of Mr. Melvin Meads, on the left, as they were entering Alamo Plaza from Avenue E, headed toward the Battle of Flowers Parade grandstands in front of the Alamo itself. Mel Meads led great bands for many years at Lee, was President of the Texas Bandmasters Association in 1967, and best of all, was my uncle.

Fiesta is a major affair each April in San Antonio and broad civic support is its foundation. This float represented Fort Sam Houston's 4th Army Headquarters Command as one of several local military installation floats. *Circa 1970, $5-7.*

Participants place wreaths of flowers in front of the Alamo as the Parade passes to honor the memories of the fallen heroes of March 1836. The main theme of the event, "Remember the Alamo," is also the title of this postcard. *Circa 1965, $4-6. Courtesy of Craig Covner.*

By 1930 tourism had become an important aspect of the city's economy and it was centered on the Alamo. Pictured is an early bus of the White Sightseeing Co. parked in front of the famous fortress or Mission #1 as it was by then known. The tour driver began his route here, then drove south to Conception or Mission #2, and onto San Jose as #3, San Juan de Capistrano #4, and then finally to San Francisco de la Espada #5. *Circa 1930, $8-10.*

This faded RPPC view is unique because it captured a time when a chimney pipe from a potbelly stove ran out a lower window leaving a lot of soot behind. The stove was in the Baptistery and must have helped take off some of the winter chill. *Circa 1909, $9-15.*
Courtesy of Martin Callahan.

Another RPPC view from about the same time shows part of the large wood frame structure built by French immigrant Honore Grenet in 1878. His two-story retail mall surrounded the old compound walls from the famous chapel to the end of the so-called long barracks. Grenet sold house wares, boots and shoes, liquors, dry goods, and "country produce" from his large store. *Circa 1907, $20-30.*
Courtesy of Martin Callahan.

A rare snowfall in San Antonio was always cause for camera owners to get busy. This rare view of a 1915 snow event shows the Alamo's courtyard under a couple inches of the white stuff. *RPPC dated March 8, 1915, $9-12.*

Beginning in 1911 the Grenet structures were finally removed from the Alamo's outer walls. This 1912 color tinted postcard shows the original long barrack's two story, limestone wall with the chapel on the far left. *Circa 1912, $7-10. Courtesy of Craig Covner.*

This bird's eye view gives a good look at the Alamo grounds as they were by World War I and before extensive restoration began. St. Paul's steeple juts above the Menger Hotel to the southeast. *Circa 1917, $7-9. Courtesy of Norman Porter.*

The Alamo-built 1718. San Antonio Texas
(Parade)

We don't know for sure what this parade was about, but can guess that it might have been for an early Battle of Flowers event. The army never wore pale blue uniforms but maybe the post card company colorist thought it looked good. A band played in front of the Alamo proper as an infantry company marched by with its officers on horseback. *Circa 1908, $6-8. Courtesy of Norman Porter.*

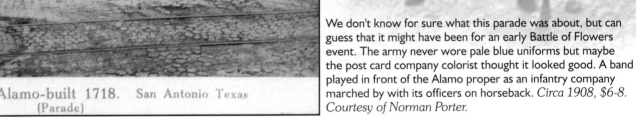

A Modern Holdup In San Antonio, Texas.

Postmarked 1911, this card was mailed out as part of a public relations campaign to attract people to San Antonio. Staging a "Modern Holdup" seems like an odd way to convince anyone that the city was indeed modern. *Circa 1912, $6-8. Courtesy of Craig Covner.*

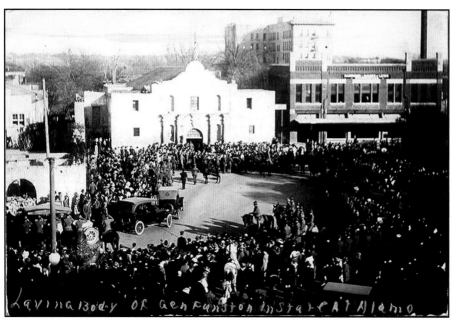

On February 19, 1917, Major General Frederick N. Funston, Commander of the Southern Department headquartered at Fort Sam Houston, San Antonio, died suddenly from a massive heart attack following dinner at the St. Anthony Hotel. He then became the first person ever to lay in state at the Alamo following the procession seen in this RPPC. Only two other people have ever had this honor, Private David B. Barkley in 1918, the U.S. Army's first Hispanic Medal of Honor recipient, and in 1945, Ms. Clara Driscoll "Saviour of the Alamo." In 1905 she put up thousands of dollars as a bond necessary to prevent the sale and demolition of the Alamo for hotel construction, thus saving it for the State of Texas and future generations. *Circa 1917, $9-12.*

Bird's Eye View of the Alamo Plaza, San Antonio, Texas

By the 1960s all Alamo postcards were in vivid color thanks to new printing techniques, inks, and papers. This "Birds Eye View" isn't that good a composition photographically, but it does show how much the old oak tree in the courtyard has grown since it was planted before World War I. *Circa 1960, $2-3. Courtesy of Norman Porter.*

The Alamo and Joskes in the background were both San Antonio traditions on Alamo Plaza for many years until the old department store was finally sold and became a Dillards property. *Circa 1965, $3-4.*

Cab #4 was a 1962 Chevrolet Biscayne belonging to the Red Ball Cab Company that was begun by Mr. Claude Talley in 1959. He attempted to compete with the older Checkered Cabs but Red Ball lasted only until 1974 before disappearing from city streets. *Circa 1963, $4-5.*

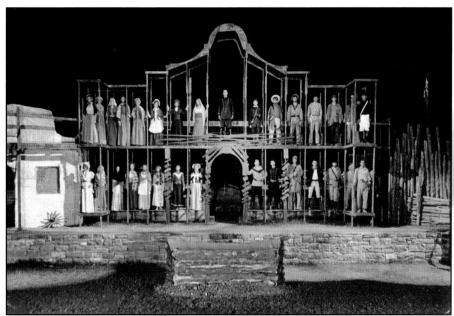

Texas playwright Ramsey Yelvington published an Alamo drama in 1959 titled "A Cloud of Witnesses" that was first performed at Baylor University in Waco. Later it was staged for a number of years as seen here at Mission San Jose. *Circa 1970, $5-7. Courtesy of Frank Thompson.*

The 1936 Texas Centennial in Dallas had its own Alamo built at 1/2 scale. The 100th birthday of Texas Fair's visitors could then tour the Alamo without traveling to San Antonio. *Circa 1936, $8-10. Courtesy of Frank Thompson.*

Of the other Alamos, the most well-known is the one built near Bracketville, Texas for the John Wayne 1960 movie "The ALAMO." His BATJAC Productions brought Mexican stonemasons to build an entire 1836 replica of San Antonio and the Alamo, which still stands. *Circa 1960, $4-5. Courtesy of Frank Thompson.*

The Alamo's classic facade has influenced local architecture for decades. An early twentieth century example was the Mission Burial Park Chapel that mimicked the Alamo facade and other mission like features. *Circa 1920, $4-5.*

The Alamo's influence on this city has been varied and powerful for many years as can be seen in this postcard. An intricately beautiful stained glass window was installed in the old Alamo National Bank lobby so as to be lit at night from inside for passersby on West Commerce Street to enjoy. *Circa 1970, $3-4. Courtesy of Craig Covner.*

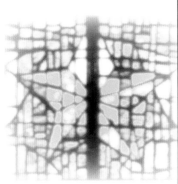

This RPPC of the Centennial replica Alamo is considered rare and valuable because of its high quality image. The attention to detail paid by its builders to the construction is obvious in this view even if not entirely accurate. *Circa 1936, $20-30. Courtesy of Frank Thompson.*

Chapter Seven:
Roadhouse Politics

San Antonio has had countless colorful characters too many to name, but this one was a character and a half in his day. He was named William "Billy" Keilman — and he was more of a force of nature than just an ordinary man. He grew up in South Bexar County on his father's ranch, several hundred acres of which eventually became Brooks Air Force Base. It was located out on the old Corpus Christi Highway, also named South Loop, for many years. As a young man, Billy joined the army that went to Cuba during the Spanish American War in 1898. Family legend says he was a Rough Rider, but his military discharge documents in the State Archives indicate a less colorful duty. Regardless, William Keilman was once a San Antonio policeman who later opened a notorious saloon/brothel "West of the Creek" near downtown, named the Beauty Bar.

Keilman's real acclaim came in 1911 when he anonymously published a guide book to the more popular haunts for local gentlemen, traveling salesmen, soldiers, or those fellows with ready cash looking for a good time. The little book had hotel, cafe, saloon, and pool hall ads plus baseball schedules, cab stand addresses and included various other services for the man about town. But its most famous feature was a listing by cost of all legal prostitutes operating in San Antonio where the profession was then licensed.

In 1917 Brooks Field was established for the flight training of hundreds of young men, so Billy opened a second club just beyond the main gate named the Horn Palace. The Palace became a very popular dinner club, dance hall, and saloon especially among the many young flying officers from nearby Brooks Field. Just like the Buckhorn downtown the Palace's walls were also covered with hundreds of animal heads and antlers as was common in watering holes of that era. Alas, one night a pair of irate patrons shot Billy on his own dance floor just as a hot jazz band had the crowd swinging and swaying. Keilman survived six bullets, but Prohibition was closing saloons by then so he sold all his horns and heads to the Buckhorn and retired. He was murdered some years later while hunting with friends, but left a lasting legacy that endures to the present day.

As previously mentioned, prostitution was licensed in San Antonio but the public's toleration of it was slowly decreasing by the time of Billy Keilman's death in the late 1930s. The military had historically sanctioned the practice, but was also becoming less tolerant of it due mostly to the high incidence of disease that was inherent in prostitution. In May 1941 a historically contentious election occurred that brought to the office of Fire and Police Commissioner a man whose job it was to finally rid the city of prostitutes. Fort Sam Houston's commanders knew that war was not far off in America's future and that San Antonio would be flooded with more troops than ever before. Social diseases caused higher rates of sick soldiers than anything else, so the city fathers demanded the end of "the oldest profession." The newly elected Police Commissioner was state Congressman Preston L. Anderson, who was very effective in overseeing the end of prostitution in San Antonio legally and otherwise.

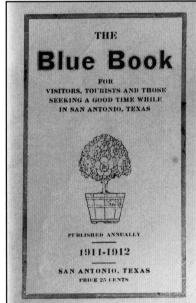

W. H. "Billy" Keilman was a notorious San Antonio character of the early twentieth century. His popular Horn Palace Bar and Cafe was at 312 East Houston Street and was a competitor of Albert's Buckhorn Saloon. Billy was a Spanish American War veteran, former city policeman, and saloonkeeper extraordinaire. Here he shows off horns well over eight feet in length of his prize long horn steer. *Circa 1915, $6-8. Courtesy of Norman Porter.*

Keilman was best known for publishing **The Blue Book**, a notorious little directory of hotels, restaurants, bars, gaming and pool parlors, and taxi cab stands downtown. It also included livery stables and cockfight venues, but most scandalous was its listing of the names and addresses of the city's many licensed prostitutes. Here, page 24 features an advertisement for Billy Keilman's own solution for too much to drink, his "Patent Plugs for Pifflicated People"; whatever it was remains a mystery. *Published 1911, $100-150.*

84

Keilman's first place was the Beauty Saloon
in the heart of the Red Light district on
Matamoros Avenue at South Concho Street.
He later opened the Horn Palace Bar &
Cafe at 312 East Houston Street. In 1916,
his father sold several hundred acres of
ranch land south of town to the Army, which
became Brooks Field flight training school.
Billy then built the larger Horn Palace Inn
across the road from Brooks Field on South
Loop, which was later named South Presa
Street. Both were in fact the old Corpus
Christi Road. *Circa 1918, $5-6. Courtesy of
Norman Porter.*

Horn Palace Inn quickly became very
popular and eventually was open only to the
Brooks Field officer corp. It was a first class
restaurant that also featured popular bands
for dancing. Keilman even ran a shuttle bus
service for his customers since the Inn was
several miles from downtown hotels. Billy
K. was shot and nearly killed on the dance
floor in 1921. *Circa 1920, $13-16.*

Like the Buckhorn, it too was decorated with
thousands of animal heads large and small
plus furniture made from hides and horns.
This view of the dining room in Keilman's
Horn Palace Bar and Cafe downtown gives
a good idea of the decor found throughout.
Distracting by today's standards, this motif
was quite common and popular a hundred
years ago mainly in German owned saloons
and eateries. *Circa 1920, $7-8.*

View Dining Room Horn Palace Bar and Cafe, San Antonio, Texas

A rare view is this RPPC showing city Commissioners being honored by twenty-two Fire Chiefs from around town. This is the only known Horn Palace card with people in the scene. *Circa 1921, $25. Courtesy of Norman Porter.*

Jack Teagarden

Seventeen year old Jack Teagarden was playing trombone with Cotton Baily and friends one night in April of 1921 at the Horn Palace when Keilman was shot on the dance floor by an angry patron. Somehow Keilman recovered, and Teagarden went on to become a legendary musician, but the Horn Palace Inn closed due to Prohibition. Keilman then sold most of his horn collection to Albert's Buckhorn downtown—where it can still be seen today. *Circa 1921, $9-12.*

The official end of San Antonio's "red light district" came in mid-1941 just as World War II was about to begin. It happened due mainly to the efforts of newly elected Fire & Police Commissioner Preston Anderson, a former state representative. An RPPC shows one of his 1943 re-election billboards at Main Street and Poplar Avenue near downtown. The still standing Aurora Apartments is seen rising above the trees on the left edge. *Dated May, 1943, $13-16. Courtesy of Fred Son.*

An election rally was held by the Victory Ticket running Preston Anderson for reelection as Fire and Police Commissioner in May of 1943. This ticket had beaten Mayor Maury Maverick in a very contentious election in May of 1941. Circa 1943, $13-16. *Courtesy of Fred Son.*

VICTORY TICKET
GUS B. MAUERMAN, MAYOR ★
PAUL STEFFLER, Street Commissioner ★
HENRY HEIN, Park Commissioner ★
P. L. ANDERSON, Fire & Police Comm. ★

VOTE FOR
P. L. ANDERSON
for FIRE *and* POLICE COMMISSIONER

To CIVILIAN SCRAP DRIVE
MAKING LAST RUN
CITY OF SAN ANTONIO
TO HELL WITH HITLER

Fire Commissioner P. L. Anderson Helps Scrap Drive, Oct. 8 1942

Fire Commissioner Preston Anderson speaks to KTSA radio listeners and a Houston Street audience during an October 1942 Scrap Drive. An 1899 city fire engine was offered up as scrap "Making Last Run" toward the war effort. *Dated October 8, 1942, $11-14. Courtesy of Fred Son.*

Chapter Eight:
The San Antonio Sound

All cities have a music history, but few have such a broad and varied assortment of sounds as have emanated from the people, places, and eras of San Antonio. America's Wild West and cowboy heritage left its own mark on the state's music. It found a home in San Antonio early on, but in a peculiarly jazzy variation known as Texas Swing—as epitomized by Bob Will and others. As with their food, Tejanos gave us a distinct and colorful flavor of music named Conjunto with Hispanic and German roots. Mix these all together and you get a unique blend that includes the Blues, Rock & Roll, Country, Tejano, and Tex Mex—and you get a Doug Sahm. Unfortunately these folks didn't really dig postcards so they are few and far between.

BLUE BONNET HOTEL - SAN ANTONIO, TEXAS

This nice linen card offers a look at the old Bluebonnet Hotel when it was home to KONO Radio as can be seen by the transmission towers on the roof. Other hotels were homes to other radio stations in the early days of broadcasting since bands, singers and touring entertainers stayed in these places. Having a radio studio in the hotel was a convenience for the performers and the stations too. *Circa 1939, $4-6.*

"Red River" Dave McEnery was one of San Antonio's most popular entertainers for decades. Born here in 1914 he became a radio, movie, and TV western singer and cowboy star. This promotional postcard came from radio station WOR in Chicago before Dave returned to San Antonio in 1949. He then starred on his own WOAI-TV show for ten years while recording many albums and making countless public appearances. *Circa 1947, $7-9.*

"RED RIVER" DAVE, Texas Troubador
RAY WINTERS, Announcer
BELL-ANS PROGRAM
WOR-MUTUAL

Musicians continued to thrive in San Antonio as large audiences heard popular bands daily over radios on stations like KTSA, WOAI, and KONO. This RPPC shows Adolph Hofner, one of San Antonio's best-loved musicians for many years. Shown left to right was pianist Bert Ferguson, Leon Seago on fiddle, Johnny Rives the drummer/fiddler, Adolph's brother Emil "Bash" Hofner with his steel guitar, Buck Wheeler on bass and Adolph himself with guitar. Known as "Adolph Hofner & the San Antonians," the band was photographed here in the KTSA broadcast studios then located in the Gunter Hotel at 205 East Houston Street. Radio stations mailed out hundreds of these postcards monthly to fans who had sent mail praising the group. *Circa 1938, $11-14. Courtesy of Andrew Brown.*

Adolph Hofner on KTSA 550 Saturdays 10-11 AM

Following World War II Adolph Hofner was hired by the PEARL Beer Company in 1949 to be their official band as was common in those days for breweries. Here is his band The Pearl Wranglers on a flat bed trailer being pulled along in San Antonio during a Battle of Flowers parade. *Circa 1955, $6-8.*

Another popular western band out of San Antonio following World War II was The Texas Top Hands, which were organized in 1946 by Walter Kleypas. In 1955 the Lone Star Brewery picked up the band, led by "Easy Adams," as its official music makers. This scene was shot at the brewery and shows "Nehi" Holley, "Easy" Adams, Jerry Shea, "Smitty" Highsmith, and others beside their 1949 Flex bus. *Circa 1954, $9-12.*

The Texas Top Hands were a popular band based in San Antonio for many years. They played all over Texas beginning in 1945 and were still performing into the 1990s. This card shows them outside the KONO radio station studios. *Circa 1954, $9-12. Courtesy of Andrew Brown.*

San Antonio's most famous female performer was Lydia Mendoza, "the queen of Tejano music." She began recording at age twelve and went on to sing and play the 12-string guitar for over sixty years. This old RPPC was used as a promotional mail out for an appearance at the old Teatro Nacional (National Theater) on West Houston Street. *Dated November 15, 1937, $14-18.*

Lydia Mendoza
15 Novembre, 1937

Teatro Nacional
San Antonio, Tx.

A modern San Antonio performer is Santiago Jimenez, Jr., well known for his enthusiastic playing of traditional Conjunto music on the accordion. Following in his famous father's path, he continues to entertain the large Tejano population of South Texas. *Dated February 1995, $3-4. Courtesy of Thomas Durnin.*

San Antonio's popular music history encompasses all styles and Jim Cullum's Happy Jazz Band was among the best known for its commitment to traditional American jazz and Dixieland. Original members seen here were Harvey Kindervater on drums, Gene McKinney trombonist, Benny Valfre played banjo, Wilson Davis, the sousaphone, Jim Cullum Jr. handled cornet, Cliff Gillette, piano with Jim Cullum Sr. on clarinet. In 1963, the band began playing nightly at The Landing, a jazz club on the River Walk. The second generation of that band, now led by Jim Cullum, Jr., still performs at The Landing today. *Circa 1964, $5-7.*

One of San Antonio's most famous musicians was Doug Sahm, who began performing as a child. He was best known for his wildly original blend of Tex-Mex, blues, Country, and rock & roll. The Texas Tornados was the Sahm band of the 1990s that entertained thousands of fans across America and in Europe too. This ad card mimicked the 1991 Zone of Our Own album cover showing band members, left to right, "Flaco" Jimenez, Augie Meyers, Freddy Fender and Doug Sahm. *Circa 1991, $3-4*

Chapter Nine:
Winging It

Aviation came early to San Antonio, making a big and lasting impression. Not long after Army aviation began at Fort Sam Houston, civil aviation followed. In fact it also began at Fort Sam, but soon moved out to the south side when a pioneering family of aviators named Stinson bought a parcel of land and opened a flight-training site. Two brothers and two sisters began Stinson Field, but it was the young girls Marjorie and Katherine who really put the place on the map and into the history books.

This art card from British artist Doug Ettridge shows the busy Stinson Field terminal at night around 1939. An American Airlines DC-3 deplanes its passengers while an Inman Brothers AT-4 Trimotor departs for take off.
Circa 1980, $8-10.

Classroom at Stinson Field

An historic South San Antonio landmark that is still in use is Stinson Municipal Airport. The flight school/aerodrome was opened in late 1915 by a family of brothers and sisters named Stinson. This makes it the second oldest continually operating flying field in America. In this view, Marjorie instructs new students in the art of flying one of the school's used B Model Wright Flyers in the fall of 1915. *Circa 1916, $15-20.*

This Mel Brown art card shows the Stinson Field terminal in the spring of 1939 when it was the city's municipal airport for the few scheduled airlines then operating in Texas. The structure was built in 1936 by President Roosevelt's employment generating Works Projects Administration or WPA. The two-story building was constructed of native sandstone and contained ticket desks, a lobby with rest area, airport management offices, and a small café much as it does today, minus ticket sales. On the bicycle is Mr. Hector Billa, the assistant airport manager at the time, who needed a bicycle to carry out his duties on the busy and expanding airfield. Hangar Six Inc. with a Pan American Airlines Ford Tri-Motor sitting inside was owned by Col. Jack Lampham. That facility provided aircraft maintenance, charter, and flight instruction for many years at Stinson including a Civilian Pilot Training Program just prior to World War II. It too still stands and provides most of the same functions today. *Circa 1996, $2-5.*

This is the only known commercially published postcard of Stinson Field, when it was officially Stinson Air Depot Training Station. It was published by the Jumbo Card Company of San Antonio. Better known for its oversized postcards Jumbo also made "Midget" Cards that were smaller than regular post cards. This card shows the WPA built, native stone Stinson Terminal during World War II when it was under Army control as an air depot. Stinson Field trained aircraft technicians, warehousemen, stores managers, and other non-combat type specialties. *Circa 1943, $9-15.*

Dr. John R. Brinkley was a regular visitor to Stinson Field during the late 1930s. The notorious "Goat Gland Doctor" from Del Rio may have been a quack but he was also an early convert to executive air travel. This Lockheed Electra 10A was his fastest and most modern aircraft, which he later sold to the Royal Canadian Air Force early in World War II. He died in San Antonio a few years later when his health and businesses failed. *RPPC circa 1938, $30-35.*

Stinson Field has had many slow years especially through the 1970s and 1980s, but is now experiencing a modern revival that continues with new construction and growth. It has hosted several air shows in the past few years like this one from about 1998. It is now officially the General Aviation reliever facility for busy San Antonio International Airport.

San Antonio International Airport, San Antonio, Texas

Following World War II the city's main airport was reestablished north of downtown off Highway 281 North and new facilities were constructed. Opened in 1953, this large, modern terminal was the heart of San Antonio International Airport for thirty years. Here a Braniff Airlines Convair 440 awaits passengers outside the busy facility. *Circa 1958, $6-8.*

Expansions kept the SATX terminal useful and busy for three more decades—well into the jet age of passenger service. In this view, a Braniff Boeing 706-720 departs San Antonio for the East Coast. *Circa 1965, $2-3.*

Best Wishes for 1960

Happy New Year from
Dee Howard Aero
San Antonio, Texas

While the SATX Terminal was busy, general and commercial aviation were also being established at the airport. The leader in that sector was Mr. Dee Howard who established an internationally renowned aircraft modification and repair business beginning in 1947. He developed a line of executive transport aircraft from surplus World War II bombers. This Christmas postcard shows a Howard Super Ventura made from a retired Navy PV-1 patrol bomber sitting in front of Howard's hangars west of the terminal. *Circa 1960, $8-10.*

A 1970s card shows the San Antonio PAX terminal as a Continental DC-8-61 Super Sixty departs "this modern new 'Jet-Port' one of the busiest in the Southwest," says the quote from the back of the card. Now known as Terminal 2 it is still in use but scheduled to be gone by 2009. *Circa 1975, $2-3.*

This nice advertising card shows a Beechcraft C-33 Debonair as it cruises over downtown San Antonio. The Debonair was one of the most successful light civil aircraft ever made and N8676Q was sold by the Beechcraft dealership at the airport. Alamo Plaza is plainly seen in this view directly beneath the aircraft. *Circa 1970, $5-7.*

According to Wikipedia, "In 2006, San Antonio International Airport handled 8,031,405 passengers, up 8 percent from 2005 and breaking the previous record of 7,437,290 set in 2005." This is the 1986 Terminal 1 and it is already beyond capacity so a new PAX structure is planned for a 2010 opening. Top image is Terminal 1, built in 1986.
Courtesy of Bob Brown.

Chapter Ten:

Uncle Sam Came to Stay

The military history of this old city since Texas became a state in 1845 is unequaled anywhere in America. Fort Sam Houston, Texas (FSH) is at once a historic and modern military installation in the heart of a major city. "Fort Sam" is known as the "Home of Army Medicine" and "Home of the Combat Medic." It is also home to Brooke General Medical Center. As of 2008, FSH is the largest and most important military medical training facility in the world. Its colorful roots are long and deep in San Antonio.

Ft. Sam Houston, Texas

Ft. Sam Houston, Texas

Fort Sam Houston was established near San Antonio in 1876 to be the central command post for a series of inner and outer frontier forts built in Texas following the civil War. This modern card shows the main gate into the original fort known as the Quadrangle. *Circa 1970, $2-3.*

Tame deer have been inside the old fort for over 120 years since they were brought in to help feed Chief Geronimo's family of Apache Indians held captive here in 1876. The historic Quadrangle encloses 8.5 acres of peaceful park surrounded by offices of the United States 5th Army. *Circa 1968, $4-5.*

This early color card shows the Government Tower that was built in 1876 on Government Hill inside the Quadrangle. The ninety-foot tall limestone tower concealed a water tank needed to supply a Quartermaster Depot originally intended for the fort. All construction including the clock tower was done with limestone cut from the nearby quarry that later became Sunken Gardens. *Circa 1907, $5-7. Courtesy of Norman Porter.*

Frank S. Thayer, Publisher, Denver

29—The Government Tower, San Antonio, Texas.

96

Across the street from the Quadrangle is the old Infantry Post main gate seen here around 1910. Future General but then Lieutenant Dwight Eisenhower and his new wife Mamie lived here in 1916. *Circa 1907, $4-5. Courtesy of Norman Porter.*

North of the Infantry Post on New Braunfels Avenue was the Artillery & Cavalry Post. Its large, open drill and parade grounds were used for unit practice and demonstrations with a horse mounted artillery battalion, as shown. *Circa 1907, $4-5. Courtesy of Craig Covner.*

Hundreds of very competent horsemen on the post met for exciting polo matches on many weekends over dozens of years. Until well after World War I there were thousands of horses and mules at Fort Sam before the Army became fully mechanized. *Circa 1912, $4-5.*

Roll Call at the Infantry Post sometime before World War I is shown here on one of many popular Fort Sam postcards of that era. *Circa 1907, $4-5.*

In 1911 the Mexican Revolution was spilling over across the Rio Grande and the Army was mobilized to secure the border. This large tent city was erected on the broad drill and parade grounds at Fort Sam. These men would soon find themselves spread along the frontier as units were assigned a certain amount of border to patrol. *Circa 1912, $4-6.*

One of the young men sent to Texas during this mobilization was eighteen-year-old Private Charles H. Meads seen here on the left. He also served on the border during the Punitive Expedition and then later in France with the 313th Infantry, 79th Division where he was severely wounded and highly decorated; he was my maternal grandfather.

Used since 1890 but formally established in 1917 for training and maneuver purposes, Camp Bullis is another historic Army post located near San Antonio. It occupies 12,000 acres on Interstate Highway 10 and Harry Wurzbach Road, seventeen miles northwest of downtown in Bexar County. The men in this old RPPC are using M1903 Springfield .30-06 bolt action rifles on one of the early ranges built at Camp Bullis. *Dated March 8, 1917. Circa 1936, $7-9; 1905, $6-8.*

This card shows the first Camp Bullis Headquarters Building during World War I when the area was far out into northwestern Bexar County. Camp Bullis is still busy training military police and other security force troops, but is now surrounded by modern-day San Antonio sprawl and development. *Dated April 28, 1917. Circa 1936, $7-9.*

By 1913 Fort Sam was the largest Army post in America and had modernized to keep abreast of emerging technology. A very significant new tool was radio communication as seen in this view of the new Wireless Radio Station on the parade grounds just east of New Braunfels Street. *Circa 1915, $4-5. Courtesy of Norman Porter.*

WIRELESS STATION, ARMY POST, SAN ANTONIO. TEX.

An art card shows the Signal Corps Aeroplane #1 depicted by this book's author, Mel Brown. Several modifications were made to it in the weeks after its arrival at Fort Sam to better the early aircraft's handling and performance. Those included the addition of wheels, a seat belt, larger gas tank for longer flights and mechanical improvements to enhance flying characteristics. Soon though aeroplanes were banned from Fort Sam because of numerous accidents, the death of Lt. George Kelly, and problems caused to Army horses and mules. *Circa 1980, $5-6.*

The Army's second aeroplane was the B Model Wright Flyer seen here in front of its hangar. The Army's first experienced pilot Lt. Benny Foulois is on the right leaning against the wing, hand on hip. *Circa 1911, $8-10.*

The Quadrangle in 1935 anchored the southern end of a big and growing installation over 3,000 acres in area. This was then the 8th Corps Area Headquarters and also where Col. Billy Mitchell was assigned in 1925. Soon after he was court-marshalled for his outspoken views on air power.
Circa 1936, $7-9. Courtesy of the Fort Sam Houston Museum.

This RPPC shows a 23rd Infantry honor guard awaiting the arrival of President Franklin Roosevelt to San Antonio on June 11, 1936. In an address at the Alamo he said "... the Alamo stands out in high relief as our noblest exemplification of sacrifice, heroic and pure." *Circa 1936, $9-15.*

Fort Sam's best-known structure is Building 1000 at the north end of the two-mile long parade grounds. Opened in 1938 as the 418-bed Station Hospital, it later became Brook Army Medical Center or BAMC. As of 2005, the building became home to U.S. Army South (USARSO) whose mission is to provide and sustain trained and ready Army forces in order to support full-spectrum military operations. *Circa 1960, $2-3.*

This card captures the lead elements of the 23rd Infantry Division (Mechanized) in 1940 only a year before the attack on Pearl Harbor and America's entry into World War II. These modernized infantry units are riding in new Dodge built, 1/2 ton, 4x4 Command Cars as the Army was trading in its pack mules and horses for gas and diesel powered vehicles in huge numbers as war loomed on the horizon. *Circa 1940, $2-3.*

BEACH PAVILION-FOURTH ARMY-FORT SAM HOUSTON, TEXAS

Built in 1939 as infantry barracks Building 2791 became surgical/convalescent hospital wards in 1943 as wounded soldiers arrived in ever increasing numbers from World War II battlegrounds. It was later named the Beach Pavilion and was my home for the entire summer of 1956 as a polio patient. *Circa 1960, $2-3. RPPC courtesy of the Fort Sam Houston Museum.*

A close-up of the West Wing of the Beach Pavilion shows the classic, Spanish Revival tan stucco common to much of Fort Sam Houston. This building is currently being restored and remodeled into modern office space after nearly sixty years as a key military medical facility. For much of that time it was home to the world renowned BAMC Burn Unit. That famous Army program is still noted as a leader in the care and treatment of the severely burned and for research into the related sciences.
Circa 1964, $2-3. Courtesy of the U.S. Army.

The Academy of Health Sciences opened on Stanley Road in 1972 as a new and important tenant at Fort Sam. At this center Army medics and allied health technicians are trained in the science and practice of military medicine. *Circa 1974, $2-3. Courtesy of the U.S. Army.*

BAMC relocated in 1996 into this state of the art military hospital on the eastern edge of Fort Sam near I-35. This structure houses a 450-bed hospital on 1.5 million square feet featuring level-one trauma care and graduate medical education. Nearly a half million Outpatients are seen annually at BAMC. *Circa 2006, $2-3. Courtesy of the U.S. Army.*

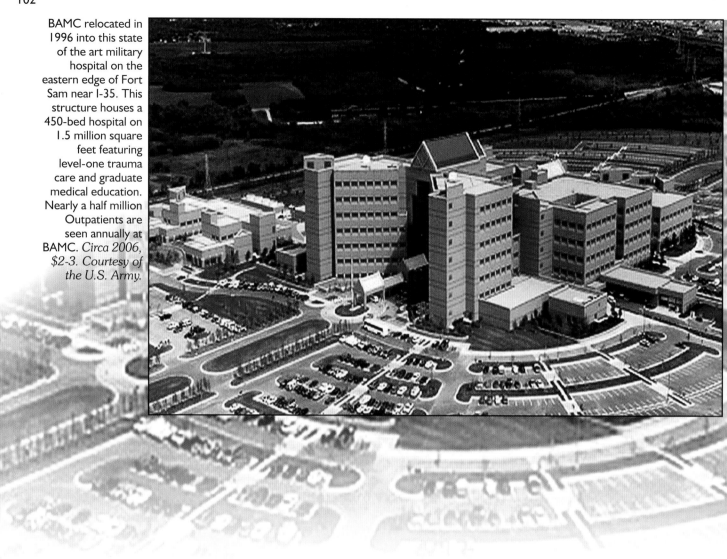

Next to BAMC is the Center For The Intrepid which is the world's most technologically advanced rehabilitation center for amputees and burn victims who have served in military operations in Iraq, Afghanistan and elsewhere. This new facility is a four-story, 65,000 square-foot site featuring two new Fisher Houses. *Circa 2006, $2-3.*

Chapter Eleven

Kelly Field

Kelly Air Force Base was the oldest continually operating air base in America until 2001 when it was "realigned" into a now city-owned facility known as Port San Antonio. Kelly's roots are long and deep going back to 1916 when it opened to train flyers for World War I. Most major historical Air Force personalities since then have been either stationed at Kelly or flew to and from it on missions. Now ninety years old, the large complex is still the site of some Air Force tenants and a major aircraft repair and modification center. It is also an air/rail point of receiving and shipping in the NAFTA Corridor.

Across town, in 1916, the Army built the first of three major flight-training sites at San Antonio. Kelly Field trained flyers for the air war in Europe in the JN-4 "Jenny" seen here. *Dated Februaray 12, 1917, $11-14. Courtesy of USAF.*

Training at Kelly brought young American men from across the nation to the art of aerial warfare. But there was also time for fun as this RPPC from the 3rd Aero Squadron baseball team shows. *Circa 1918, $13-16.*

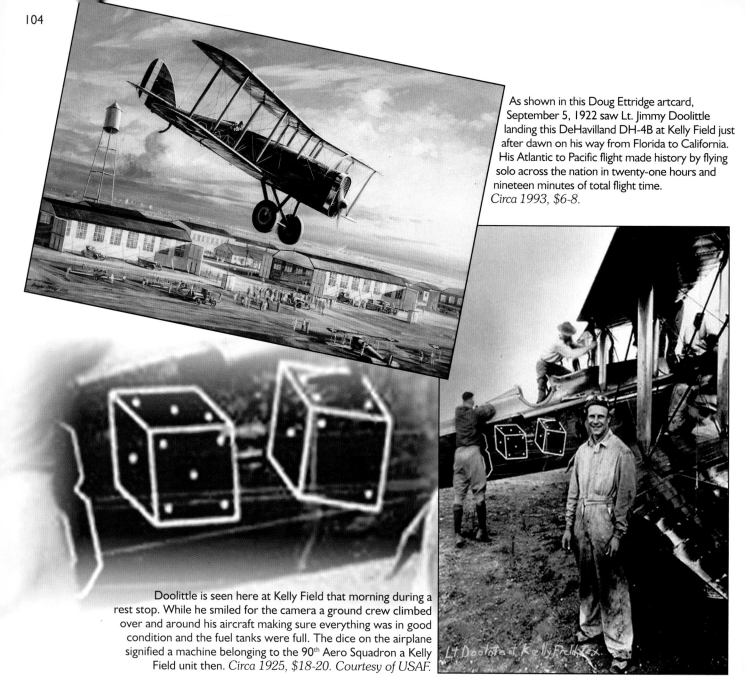

As shown in this Doug Ettridge artcard, September 5, 1922 saw Lt. Jimmy Doolittle landing this DeHavilland DH-4B at Kelly Field just after dawn on his way from Florida to California. His Atlantic to Pacific flight made history by flying solo across the nation in twenty-one hours and nineteen minutes of total flight time. *Circa 1993, $6-8.*

Doolittle is seen here at Kelly Field that morning during a rest stop. While he smiled for the camera a ground crew climbed over and around his aircraft making sure everything was in good condition and the fuel tanks were full. The dice on the airplane signified a machine belonging to the 90th Aero Squadron a Kelly Field unit then. *Circa 1925, $18-20. Courtesy of USAF.*

Almost twenty years later, a flight of cadet solos are shown in a North American BC-1 trainer from the 61st School Squadron at Kelly Field in 1940. America was beginning to ramp up its air force since war had begun in Europe a year earlier. *Circa 1940, $8-10.*

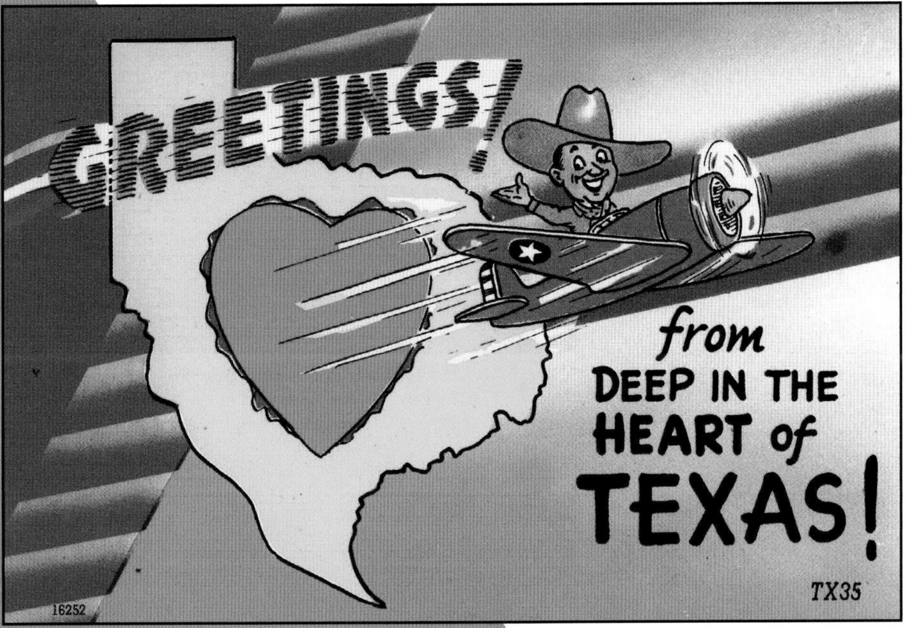

Comic cards like this one were popular during World War II's early years. This one was mailed in July 1942 from Kelly Field, which was only one of the sixty-five Army Air Fields in Texas then. *Circa 1942, $3-4.*

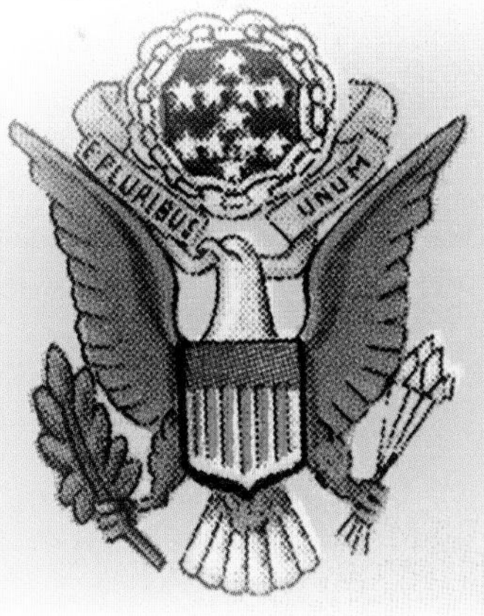

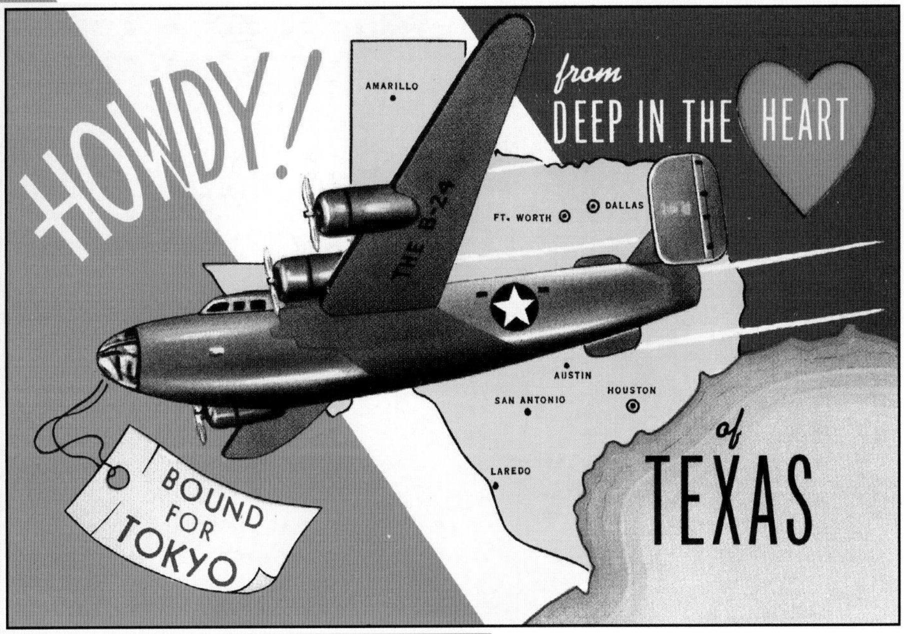

Another fun card from "Deep in the Heart of Texas" offers a serious note attached to the B-24's nose. A total of 18,482 Liberator bombers were built during World War II including hundreds in two Texas plants; one at Dallas, another at Fort Worth. ***Circa 1941, $4-5.***

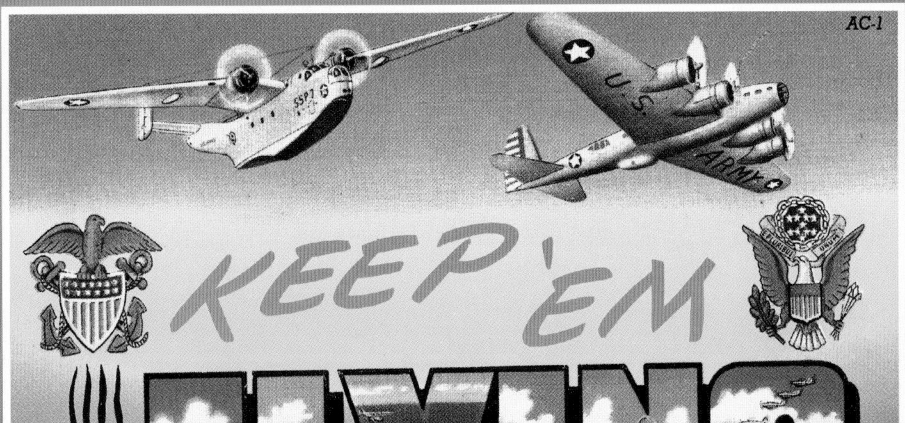

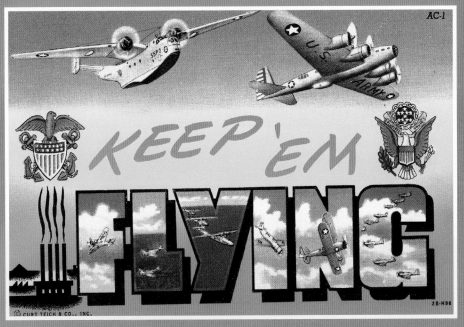

This colorful postcard was first published in 1940 before America entered World War II. It remained a popular card that featured the much-used patriotic phrase "KEEP 'EM FLYING" in large letters. In pristine condition like this one they are still a favorite among collectors. ***Circa 1941, $3-4.***

Kelly Field just before World War II began was busy training new pilots in four different specialties needed for the coming conflict. Based upon certain skills and aptitudes, the young flyers were chosen to become fighter, bomber, attack or reconnaissance pilots. This long flight line became busier as the war became more inevitable. *Circa 1940, $3-5.*

28:—KELLEY FIELD, SAN ANTONIO AIR DEPOT, SAN ANTONIO, TEXAS

This postcard view was shot at Kelly Field, but the scene could have been found at any military flying field. They all used parachutes that required drying and repacking after occasional use and cleanings. *Circa 1943, $3-4.*

35—Packing Parachutes at U.S. Air Fields, San Antonio, Texas

During World War II Kelly Field ended its long time flight-training when it became a major modification and repair installation for the Air Force. In 1949 the giant Convair B-36 "Peacemaker" began its ten-year USAF career that had them flying in and out of Kelly Air Force Base regularly. This popular card shows an early A model that did not have the outboard jet engines that were added later. *Circa 1956, $5-6.*

A one of a kind aircraft that graced the skies over San Antonio from Kelly Air Force Base was this behemoth, the XC-99. With a wingspan of 230 feet and 185 feet in length, it was the cargo version of the B-36. Only one was ever built, being designed toward the end of WW II as a means to carry fifty ton loads across the Pacific. Stationed at Kelly in 1950, it flew limited missions for the San Antonio Air Depot until July 1957 when it was retired. It sat for the next fifty years gradually decaying until being moved to the Air Force Museum in 2005 for restoration at the Ohio facility. *Circa 1950, $3-4*

Open House 1960 at Kelly Air Force Base was crowded as always for the annual Armed Forces Day event held the third Sunday each May beginning in 1949. Here the masses mill around a Strategic Air Command B-47 Stratojet that provided some shade on those blistering hot end of May weekends. A few hundred acres of sun-heated concrete were dangerously radiant by mid afternoon but getting up close to American Air Power was worth it. *Circa 1960, $6-8.*

Another view from that same weekend, this time showing an F-102A Delta Dagger (left) and an F-100D Super Sabre. Both were Tactical Air Command, "Century Series" fighters of the Cold War era. Those yearly Open House days were and are always heavily attended pubic events as San Antonio is very proud of its historic military heritage. Air power displays were staged out along the main runways with high-speed jet passes and napalm scorching the grassy areas in between. These sleek war birds were also the source for occasional and startling "sonic booms" over town before they were banned in the early 1960s. *Circa 1960, $6-8.*

A truly stunning sight was this first production model B-58 Hustler that came to Kelly AFB in March 1960 for use as a training aid. Kelly's maintenance teams were responsible for the care and support of the Strategic Air Command's B-58 fleet during the unique aircraft's short, six year long USAF career. One B-58 was the star of the 1960 Armed Forces Day air show as it made low, high speed passes down the long runways. *Circa 1960, $4-5. Courtesy of USAF.*

The original seven Mercury astronauts regularly flew into Kelly during the 1960s for medical evaluations at nearby Brooks AFB School of Aerospace Medicine. Here they pose by an F-106B Delta Dart at Kelly, L to R, Deke Slayton, Gordo Cooper, John Glenn, Gus Grissom, Wally Schirra, Alan Shepard, and Scott Carpenter. *Circa 1962, $7-8.*

The mid 1960s and early 1970s were the busiest years since World War II at Kelly, particularly for the San Antonio Air Depot or SAAD. Due to the war in Vietnam, repair work, modifications and upgrades were done on dozens of the B-52 Stratofortresses as seen in this card from about 1966. *Circa 1967, $5-7. Courtesy of USAF.*

"World's Largest Hangar" was no joke since Building #375 was a 2,000 feet long and 300 feet wide hangar with over a million square feet of floor space. Kelly Air Force Base's bread and butter from 1954 to 1995 was the Boeing B-52 Stratofortress and this hangar could hold several of them simultaneously. *Circa 1960, $5-6.*

Beginning in 1960 these C-119 Flying Boxcars of the 433rd Troop Carrier Wing were stationed across the long runways from Kelly at the Air Force Reserve site. The USAFRES "Alamo Wing" was part of the very critical, emergency airlift activity prompted by the "Cuban Missile Crisis" of October 1962. *Circa 1965, $2-3. Courtesy of the USAF.*

As the war in Vietnam went on, Kelly became an aerial port for the shipment of large amounts of equipment and supplies needed in theater. This aging C-124 Globemaster, known as "Old Shakey" due to its vibrations, is seen at Kelly about 1965. It was being fed a support vehicle and several thousand tons of other items for transport to Southeast Asia. *Circa 1965, $6-8. Courtesy of the USAF.*

One very special "Buff" visited the SAAD in August of 1986 for its IRAN (Inspect & Repair As Necessary). This was B-52B #52-0008 NASA "Mothership" from Edwards AFB. Ca. "Balls Eight" was used to launch many types of Experimental aircraft beginning with its 1960 flights carrying aloft the X-15 "rocket plane." She was finally retired on December 17, 2004 after forty-four years of duty and now sits at the Edwards AFB main gate.

During the 1980s and early 1990s another special visitor to Kelly was the unique NASA Boeing 747 carrying the various Space Shuttles. After a mission the space ships landed at Edwards AFB and were carried back to Cape Canaveral in Florida. Big crowds always gathered at Kelly to watch the "Piggy-Back" pair stop for refueling. *Circa 1995, $2-3. Courtesy of the USAF.*

Here the special NASA 747 and its famous cargo, the Shuttle Columbia, receive last minute inspection and care by Kelly teams before they depart for the second leg of their trip to Cape Canaveral, Florida. Kelly AFB's extra long runways made it one of the designated stopping points for these transcontinental flights.
Circa 1995, $2-3. Courtesy of the USAF.

An Air Force Reserve, 433rd Airlift, "Alamo Wing" C-5 Galaxy greets another South Texas sunrise at Kelly Field Annex. Across from Port San Antonio, formerly Kelly AFB, the Air Force has established its C-5 Formal Training Unit. Since 2006 all C-5 crews must pass through this school before being assigned to the Galaxy.
Circa 2002, $2-3. Courtesy of the USAF.

Sharing the Kelly Field Annex space with C-5s at Lackland is the Texas Air National Guard's Lone Star Gunfighters of the 182nd Fighter Squadron/149th Fighter Wing. The fighter wing is part of the US Air Forces Air Education and Training Command (AETC) and is one of the primary "school houses" for F-16 pilots.
Circa 2002, $2-3. Courtesy of the USAF.

The Gunfighters on this card owned Block 30 F-16C/D Fighting Falcons built by Lockheed at Fort Worth.
Circa 2002, $2-3. Courtesy of the USAF.

Chapter Twelve:
Brooks Field

Brooks Air Force Base was the second oldest military flight training site built near San Antonio during World War I. It is still there, but Brooks has also evolved into a mixed-use facility now sharing its space with municipal and private commercial ventures as well as some Air Force assets. Brooks too has been home to famous airmen throughout its history from Charles Lindbergh to "Tex" Hill. Since the 1960s Brooks has served America's NASA astronaut program with its School of Aerospace Medicine.

Brooks Air Force Base sat on San Antonio's South side for nearly ninety years after being built in 1917 during World War I. This modern postcard was the last one published before the old base was "Realigned" into Brooks City Base. *Circa 2002, $2-3.*

Another of the author's art cards shows a JN-4 Jenny taking off at Brooks Field on a busy day in April 1917 during World War I. The training schedule was packed with dual instruction and solo flights while Brooks Field tried to produce as many capable new pilots as possible. *Circa 1995, $3-4.*

Built in December 1917, this World War I hangar at Brooks is the last of its kind remaining in the Air Force. It is the Hangar 9 Edward White Museum named for the San Antonio astronaut killed in a fire in 1967 at Cape Canaveral. *Circa 2006, $2-4. Courtesy of the USAF.*

One of Brooks Fields earliest tenants was the Lighter Than Air or LTA School for three years beginning in 1919. Here is the ill-fated Army Blimp C-2 that stopped at Brooks to refuel in April of 1922. Behind it can be seen part of the huge blimp hangar built to house such gas filled behemoths. *Dated April, 1922, $16-20.*

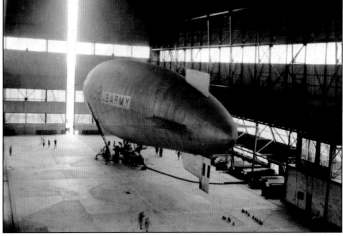

The C-2 was moved inside the hangar for safety, but was to be taken out the next morning. This rare RPPC shows the big balloon in its last few moments of existence before being moved out of the hangar. When it was being towed from the hangar a gust of wind blew the C-2 against the hangar door causing a tear and the blimp was destroyed. *Circa 1922, $16-20. Courtesy of Preston Son.*

36 BROOKS FIELD, SAN ANTONIO, TEXAS

PHOTO BY U. S. ARMY AIR CORPS

5A-H1610

This common but wonderful postcard shows early parachute trials at Brooks Field in September 1929. The blimp hangar can be seen at the left edge while just above the center parachute can be seen the freshly laid gravel runways at nearby Stinson Field. This particular image is a good example of how careful examination of an old and familiar postcard can yield details of history sometimes forgotten otherwise. *Circa 1930, $3-4.*

This RPPC was shot the same day and probably by the same cameraman as the parachute demonstration unfolded. It is one of my favorite views because just below the tail of airplane #332 is the notorious – but by then defunct – Horn Palace owned by Billy Keilman. The Palace and its distinctive driveway off South Loop Road can clearly be seen since the jump aircraft were directly above Brooks field for the demonstration. *Dated September 3, 1929, $18-20.*

Brooks Field· Tx.
9·3·29 Parachute Demonstration

Ready to Solo-Wish Me Luck

"Ready To Solo— Wish Me Luck," the sender wrote on this RPPC for mailing to family and friends. This particular card had a less optimistic note on the back to a friend who had already "washed out" at Brooks. The young man leaning on the deep blue Consolidated PT-1 trainer #444 predicted that he too might fail his solo flight. Actually the PT-1 was fairly forgiving so our subject likely passed this stage of instruction. *Circa 1933, $8-10.*

Field·Tx.

Brooks Field-Tex.
Blimp Hangar
Sept. 9, 1941

This huge blimp hangar was built at Brooks in 1919 for the Army Balloon School when those gas bags were still seen as effective for reconnaissance work. Its giant doors were moved back and forth on railroad tracks with large electric motors. Like all structures of this size, rain could actually fall inside as a result of warmth and high humidity.
Dated September 9, 1941, $8-10.

29:-HANGARS, QUARTERS AND DIRIGIBLE HANGAR
BROOKS FIELD. SAN ANTONIO. TEXAS

This card also shows the uniquely elliptical hangar line at Brooks Field as a student pilot cruises in a BC-1 over the old blimp hangar still standing by the beginning of World War II. By this time Brooks had paved runways rather than the open landing "fields" as before that were dangerous in wet weather. *Circa 1941, $3-4.*

116

Pilot training remained Brooks' main role during World War II, but that ended with the Allied Victory. Brooks then became home to Air Force Reserve and Texas Air National Guard units. This 1954 aerial view shows the parking ramp full of F-51 Mustangs belonging to the 182nd Fighter Wing and assorted other aircraft. *Circa 1950, $3-4.*

BROOKS AIR FORCE BASE, TEXAS

One of that unit's F-84Gs was named the San Antonio Rose after the popular Bob Wills, Texas Swing song. While at Brooks the 182nd flew World War II era F-51 Mustangs but went to the Korean War in new jet fighters. *Circa 1952, $8-10. Courtesy Floyd Prozanski.*

The war in Korea took units like the 182nd Fighter Squadron from Brooks Air Force Base to serve during the conflict. This old Kodachrome card shows F-84 pilots discussing a mission. *Circa 1953, $5-6.*

In 1959 Brooks AFB became home to a very important new tenant, The School of Aerospace Medicine. Founded in 1922 the unit is tasked with all aspects of flight medicine. In particular the Brooks campus was charged with overseeing the health of America's newest aviation heroes, the astronauts of the space program. *Circa 2002, $2-3. Courtesy of USAF.*

"West Point of the Air"

When it opened in 1930 Randolph Field was known as the "West Point of the Air" because it was the main site for undergraduate pilot and commissioned officer training akin to the Army's real West Point in New York. Since then it has continued to train young Americans to be the best pilots possible when serving and protecting their nation. Since it became Randolph Air Force Base in 1947, the picturesque training center has specialized in producing instructor pilots. Beginning in 1974 RAFB has also been home to the 562nd Flying Training Squadron that produces new flight navigators for the Air Force.

Perhaps San Antonio's most famous base is its historic Randolph AFB or Field, as it was originally known. This classic "Large Letter" card is a pre-World War II example of Americana. *Circa 1941, $5-6.*

Beginning with its opening in June 1930, "West Point of the Air" was Randolph's nickname for over twenty-five years. This album type card gathered scenes from all around the installation to give the viewer plenty to look at. *Circa 1941, $5-6.*

Another hard to find RPPC, it shows the 1929 construction of Randolph's main administration site Building 100 or the Taj Mahal as it came to be known. Less known is that the Taj has always hidden a half million-gallon water tank seen here before being walled in.
Circa 1929, $16-20.
Courtesy of USAF.

This special shot of the Taj appeared on a Jumbo Card Company item in 1935. Atop the tiled dome was a temporary wood platform built for a camera crew from Hollywood at Randolph to film "West Point of the Air." The movie featured Robert Young, Wallace Berry and Maureen O'Sullivan but the real star was a young Randolph Field itself.
Circa 1935, $5-6.

Due to the unique design and beauty of Randolph's physical appearance, more postcards were made of it through the years than were ever done for any other air base anywhere. This aerial view captures that wagon wheel plan that is so recognizable.
Circa 1935, $3-4.

These prewar training plane colors were very distinctive for a good reason. Sometimes there were several dozen of these BC-1 aircraft in the air over Randolph daily so they needed to be highly visible to prevent collisions. *Circa 1939, $3-4.*

"Take Off" Instead of "Forward March" is the title of this familiar card that was likely sent home by the hundreds annually by the many cadets passing through Randolph's basic flight school. *Circa 1939, $2-3.*

This distinctive card features a central view from Randolph Field as it's surrounded, dreamlike, by other late 1930s Air Corps aircraft. It was published in different versions with various base names on the frame. *Circa 1939, $5-7.*

120

This obviously staged scene came from Randolph Field during World War II and was probably a popular item. The card back caption reads: "Staff Sergeant Boots, the Texas Ranger of Randolph Field, is shown here wearing pistols and M.P. band ... Said Sergeant Boots with a loud yap; 'It'll be worse than yaps for the Japs if they show up on my post.'" *Circa 1942, $3-4*

Aircraft traffic controllers stand on an outside balcony to direct dozens of trainers manned by cadets. An otherwise normal looking postcard image is made more dramatic by its mailing date as noted in pencil at the card's top. It was sent on December 6, 1941, the day before the Japanese attacked Pearl Harbor, causing America to enter World War II. Randolph's already busy training schedule soon got even busier as the demand for trained Army Air Corps pilots jumped higher than ever before. *Circa 1942, $3-4.*

This hangar line photograph was originally shot in black & white and then colorized. Oddly it was not done completely since the checkerboard roofs were painted black and yellow back then. *Circa 1939, $3-4.*

During World War II the main mission for Randolph Field changed from basic flight training to instructor pilot training. The Air Force desperately needed trained instructors to teach the thousands of men needed to pilot the dozens of different type aircraft then being operated. Instructor training remained the base's main mission after World War II's end. This "Plastichrome" from Randolph about 1950 shows that the trustworthy T-6 Texan was still producing able instructors for the Air Force. *Circa 1950, $6-8.*

This four-ship flight of T-37B "Tweets" flying from Randolph (tail code RA) exemplifies the capable skills needed by Air Force instructor pilots. Tweets are said to be among the world's most pilot friendly jet airplanes and has been flying in the U.S. Air Force since 1957. *Circa 2005, $3-4.*

The highly reliable Tweet served as the primary pilot instructor training aircraft at Randolph from October 1965 until April 2007. This view shows the last T-37B departing from the historic air base. In almost forty-two years of operation there, 7,737 instructor pilots graduated from Randolph thanks to the Tweety Bird. *Circa 2007, $3-4.*

Pilots moved from the T-37 up to this sleek trainer, the T-38A Talon. It is a supersonic jet that was introduced into Air Force use in March 1961 and is seen here passing over Randolph in the early 1970s. *Circa 1973, $6-8.*

Replacing the venerable Tweet, this is the newest pilot trainer to call Randolph AFB home, a T-6A Texan II built by the Beech Aircraft Company. The turboprop Texan IIs began arriving in the 12th FTW's squadrons in May 2000 and are gradually being upgraded to T-6B status. *Circa 2005, $3-4.*

Another training aircraft familiar to Randolph since 1974 is the T-43 Gator, a converted Boeing 737 transport. The primary mission of Randolph's 12 T-43s is navigator training. The Gator has stations for twelve navigator students, six instructors, plus pilot and copilot flight crew. This lovely view of a T-43 from Randolph's 562nd Flying Training Squadron shows it banking toward downtown San Antonio in a very postcard proper pose. *Circa 2005, $3-4.*

Howdy From Randolph Air Force Base, TX.

North American T-38 Talon

Talons are still very much in use at Randolph AFB for the Air Education and Training Command's 12th Flying Training Wing. This Talon is a new T-38C, which began coming into the 12th FTW's five squadrons at Randolph in January 2004. *Circa 2007, $3-4.*

Chapter Fourteen:
Aviation Cadet Center/ Lackland AFB

BC-1 TRAINERS IN ECHELON

The San Antonio Aviation Cadet Center (SAACC) opened as World War II was beginning, due to the need for larger than ever numbers of trained crew for the Air Force. Sited adjacent to Kelly Field it grew quickly and after the war became Lackland Air Force Base.

Following the birth of the United States Air Force in 1947 as a separate uniformed military service, Lackland AFB eventually became the first home to new airmen. As the "Gateway to the Air Force" and home to the 37th Training Wing, Lackland is where all new recruits receive basic military training for the aerospace component of America's armed forces. The large base is also home to various tenants including some Air Force schools, the Sentry Dog Training Branch, and the Air Force Intelligence, Surveillance, and Reconnaissance Agency. Lackland's best-known family member beyond the USAF Gateway is Wilford Hall Medical Center, home to the 59th Medical Wing, the largest hospital in the Air Force.

This interesting view of a perfect formation T-6 Texans out of the SAACC is misleading. Pilot training was not a function of the SAACC; rather its sole purpose was to determine which cadets were best suited for which specialty. Then they were sent to flight school, or one for navigators, bombardiers, gunners, mechanics, or the infantry if they showed no ability to fly in any capacity. This remains a popular card. *Circa 1942, $4-5.*

"NEW GUESTS" ARRIVING AT SAN ANTONIO AVIATION CADET CENTER

Far across town is another unique Air Force installation that can trace its roots back to World War II. Thousands of young American's were then entering the Air Force with dreams of becoming pilots. One main processing site was deemed best to select those most suitable for flight crews and so the San Antonio Aviation Cadet Center was born in early 1942. *Circa 1942, $3-4.*

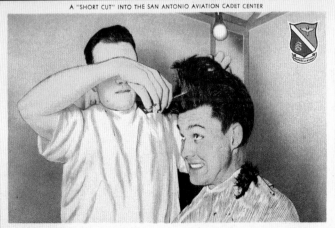

A "SHORT CUT" INTO THE SAN ANTONIO AVIATION CADET CENTER

A series of postcards were produced to tell the SAACC story beginning with the previous one, which shows the recruits coming off the train. Next was this one of a new cadet getting the mandatory "GI" (government issue) haircut. *Circa 1942, $3-4.*

By this stage, the new cadets were in uniform and had been issued a duffle bag filled with their new GI clothing, kit, and personal items. Here they are waiting to be processed into the next phase of testing, selection and assignment. *Circa 1942, $3-4.*

ON ARRIVAL AT SAN ANTONIO AVIATION CADET CENTER, SAN ANTONIO, TEXAS

"GETTING ON TO THE ROPES"

Keeping fit and increasing the physical aptitudes of the new cadets was a priority at the SAACC. These men are running the physical conditioning course. *Circa 1942, $3-4.*

Greetings from **LACKLAND AIR FORCE BASE** San Antonio Texas

The Gateway to the Air Force

In 1948, the SAACC was renamed Lackland Air Force Base to honor Brigadier General Frank Lackland. He originated the concept of a single recruit-processing center for the Air Force. Since then Lackland AFB has been "The Gateway to the Air Force." This is where all new recruits receive Basic Military Training (BMT) before going on to specialty and technical schools. *Circa 1970, $4-5.*

A big part of Air Force basic training is organized around arduous physical activity designed to enhance self-esteem. This card shows part of the late 1960s Confidence Course at Lackland. *Circa 1970, $4-5.*

Day after day for the first few weeks at Lackland the new recruits learn good old fashion soldiering the Air Force way, which is done on the drill ground. Regimentation is the key to military philosophy, which means becoming units rather than a group of individuals and this is where it is taught. Wilford Hall Hospital can be seen in the background. *Circa 1970, $4-5.*

This familiar card shows a USAF officer discussing the static displayed F-80 Shooting Star to a group of foreign military officers. They were enrolled at Lackland's Defense Language Institute English Language Center (DLIELC). This school has taught English to allied military nationals since 1954. The F-80 is one of thirty-nine permanently displayed historic aircraft at Lackland. *Circa 1955, $4-5.*

126

From 1948 to 1975 women were trained separately at Lackland to become members of the Women in the Air Force or WAFs. They now go through BMT as regular service members since women have been fully integrated into the Air Force. This group of WAFs is seen marching downtown on Broadway as part of the Battle of Flowers Parade in the late 1950s. *Circa 1957, $4-5.*

The History & Traditions Museum opened November 6, 1956, as a BMT Air Force history classroom in a remodeled 1942 processing center. The Matador Missile is no longer out front but other historic aircraft are still displayed there. *Circa 1965, $4-5.*

Wilford Hall is the largest Air Force Hospital in the world with fifteen clinical and surgical specialty departments. In 2007 during a typical 24-hour day, there were 2,658 patient visits, 9,442 prescriptions dispersed, forty patients admitted, thirty-five surgeries performed, six babies delivered, 9,285 lab procedures done, and 2,600 meals served. *Circa 1975, $4-5.*

Home of the 59th Medical Wing, USAF

Wilford Hall Medical Center
Lackland Air Force Base, Tx.

32: THE ALAMO BY NIGHT, SAN ANTONIO, TEXAS

Bibliography

Bowser, David. *West of the Creek; Murder, Mayhem and Vice in Old San Antonio.* San Antonio, Texas: Maverick Publishing Company, 2003.

Brown, Mel. *Chinese Heart of Texas: the San Antonio Community, 1875 to 1975.* Austin, Texas: Lily on the Water Publishing, 2005.

San Antonio in Vintage Postcards. Chicago, Illinois: Arcadia Publishing, 2000.

Wings Over San Antonio. Chicago, Illinois: Arcadia Publishing, 2000.

Cagle, Eldon. *FORT SAM; The Story of Fort Sam Houston, Texas.* San Antonio, Texas: Maverick Publishing, 2003.

Fisher, Lewis. *Crown Jewell of Texas; The Story of the San Antonio River.* San Antonio, Texas: Maverick Publishing, 1997.

"Franklin D. Roosevelt XXXII President of the United States 1933-1945 #69 Address at the Alamo, San Antonio, Texas. June 11th, 1936." http://www.presidency.ucsb.edu/ws/index.php?pid=15299

"HemisFair'68" http://en.wikipedia.org/wiki/HemisFair_'68

Leatherwood, Art. "Camp Bullis." http://www.tsha.utexas.edu/handbook/online/articles/CC/qbc6.html

Manguso, John. *The Post at San Antonio, Fort Sam Houston 1845-1879.* San Antonio, Texas: Fort Sam Houston Museum, 2002.

A Pictorial History of Kelly Air Force Base. San Antonio, Texas: Office of History, San Antonio Air Logistics Center, Kelly Air Force Base, Texas, 1984.

"San Antonio Japanese Tea Gardens." http://en.wikipedia.org/wiki/San_Antonio_Japanese_Tea_Gardens

"The History of Fiesta San Antonio." http://www.fiesta-sa.org/history.aspx

"The San Antonio River Native American Uses and European Discovery." http://www.edwardsaquifer.net/sariver.html

Thompson, Frank T. *The Alamo.* San Diego, California: Thunder Bay Press, 2002.

The Star Film Ranch: Texas' First Picture Show. Plano, Texas: Republic of Texas Press, 1996.

Underwood, John. *The Stinsons; A Pictorial History.* Glendale, California: Heritage Press, 1976

Wings Over San Antonio. Arcadia Publishing, 2001.

Woolford, Sam and Bess. *The San Antonio Story.* San Antonio, Texas: The Steck Company, 1950.

Index